***Dreams of the return***

# *Dreams of the return*

Alan Bern

Quali fioretti dal notturno gelo
chinati e chiusi, poi che 'l sol li 'mbianca,
si drizzan tutti aperti in loro stelo,

tal mi fec'io di mia stanca

Night's freeze, those florets bent over and closed up,
even the littlest ones, muscular, stand
in bright, white sunlight on their stems, all opened,

as I, my worthiness now weary, stood straight up

Dante, Inferno II, 127-130

OLD SCRATCH PRESS | LOS ANGELES

Published by Old Scratch Press, an imprint of Current Words Publishing, LLC.
Printed and manufactured in the United States of America

ISBNs
978-1-957224-90-9 (paperback)
978-1-957224-57-2 (epub)

oldscratchpress.com
currentwords.com

thanks to my old friends, great friends

Artist and printer Robert Woods who has taught me more about combining words and images than I can put into words

Poet and educator Marco Rossi-Doria, buon amico e bravo ragazzo, who has schooled me over the years about his city Napoli and his country Italia

Peter Truskier, who perfected the layout for this book and made it match my desires and intentions and those of my publishers as well

and my love and thanks to my wife Alice
for our voyages to Italia
and for her ever-daily support of my work
ti bacio, ti bacio, amore mio

**ALSO BY ALAN BERN**

No no the saddest (Fithian Press, 2004)

Waterwalking in Berkeley (Fithian Press, 2007)

IN THE PACE OF THE PATH, (UnCollected Press, 2023)

because lack (back room poetry, 2024)

***Dreams of the return***

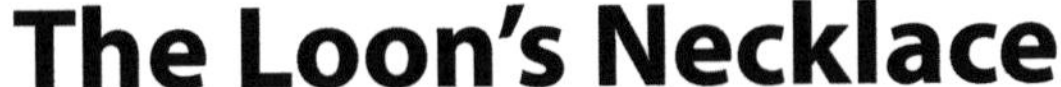

# The Loon’s Necklace

# The Loon's Necklace

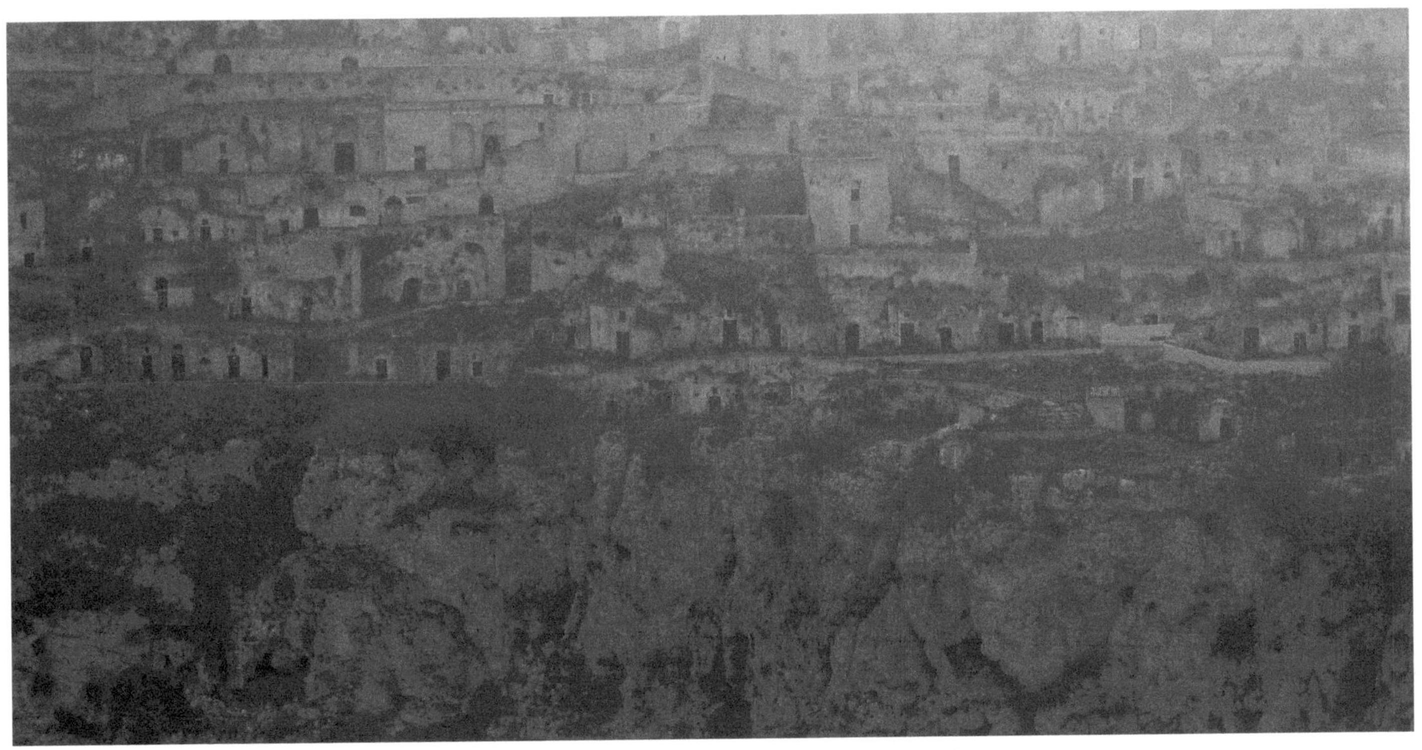

Matera: in the Sassi, ancient caves where humans resided for over 9,000 years.
Was the ravine (la gravina) below too dry for loons?

Matera, 1955

"In the 1950s Matera was a slum city. Tens of thousands of people lived in the Sassi in unhygienic troglodyte conditions [in caves, often with livestock], and malaria was prevalent. The prime minister at the time declared it was 'Italy's shame'."
BBC News, http://news.bbc.co.uk/2/hi/europe/4616480.stm

I

What does she cook
Woman from the Caves
her world is
the small round fountain
waterless

there she watches children,
darning, talks to those who pass
then circles clockwise and counter
where she swept earlier

where does she cook and what

II

among the rocks, Caves,
on these stones, her feet bare
in the Sassi she has walked and walked

yes, the tufa is soft, but her feet
callused so that she gains height
walking and the cracks never mend

everything here is parched
even the cries are parched

[Maybe the ravine once contained water enough
to welcome loons in these many thousand years?
The tremolo calls of the Woman from the Caves.]

Caves are eyes
in my memory—
Matera, 1965

Tell, what figures
from the entrance,
what sits inside the cavern—
not blue this grotto,
not light this cave
opening.

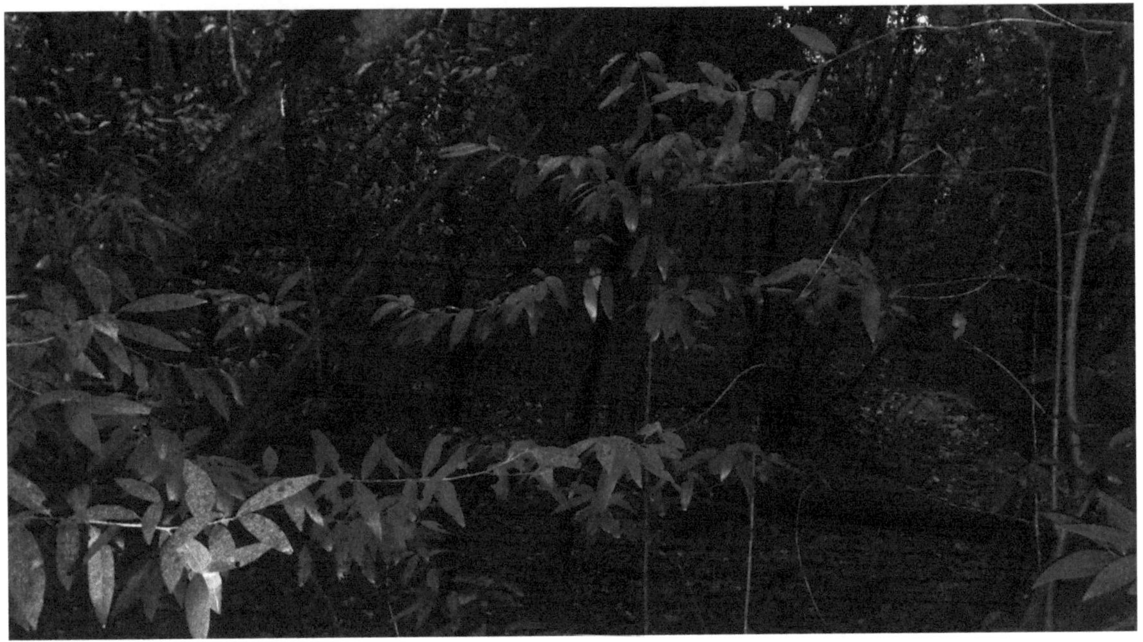

[Then a new dream arrives to her,
Woman from the Caves, in the early morning
filled with the wavering sounds of loons hunting.
Awakening there is ample evidence of blood.]

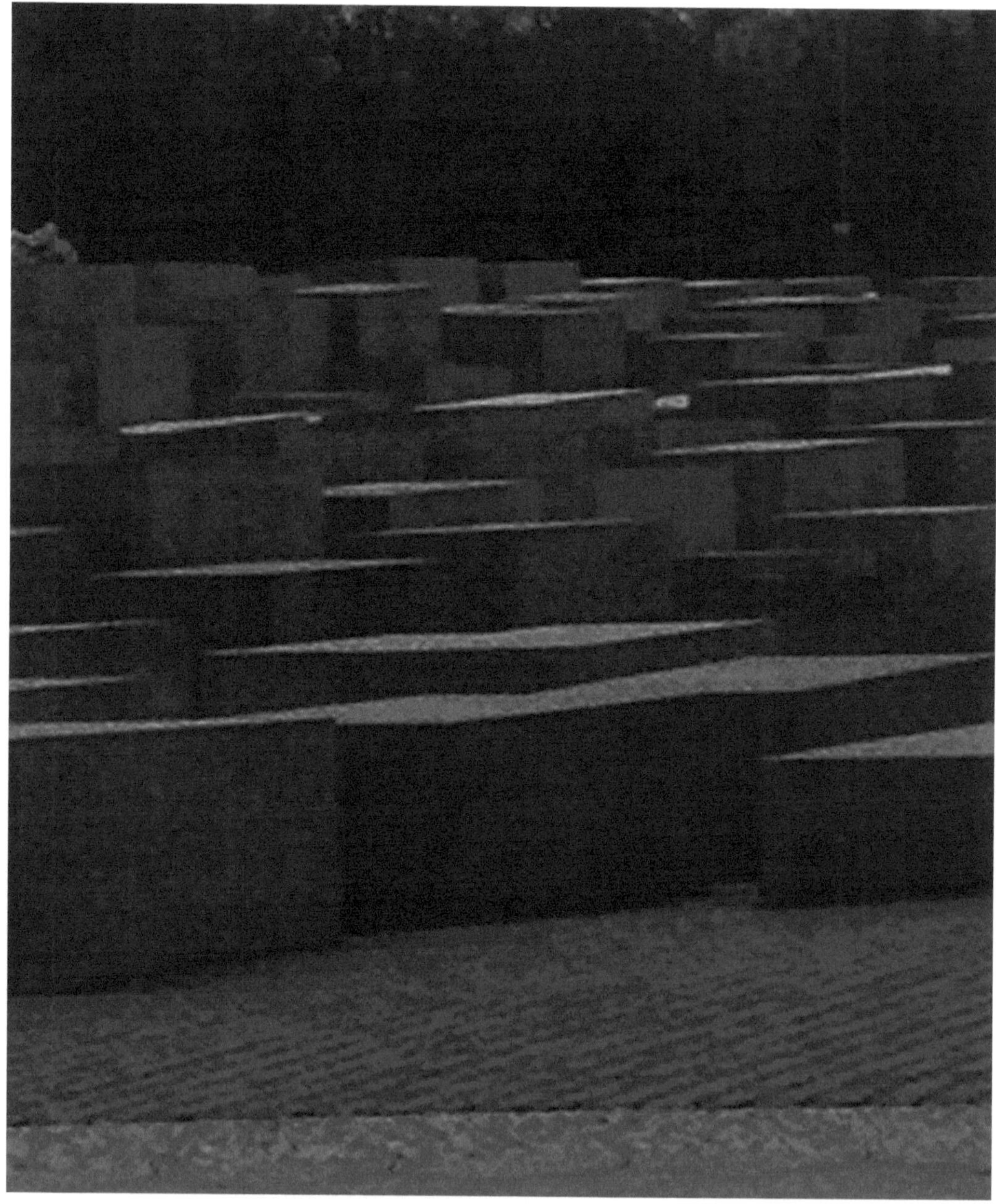

## when the loon's necklace is brutally removed

I've this necklace for you,
Mother!

Where have you found it, Boy?
And why does it bleed onto my hands?

It is from the loon, Mother.

Boy! There are no loons nearby, you know that.
What do you tell me?  You do recall my trouble seeing?

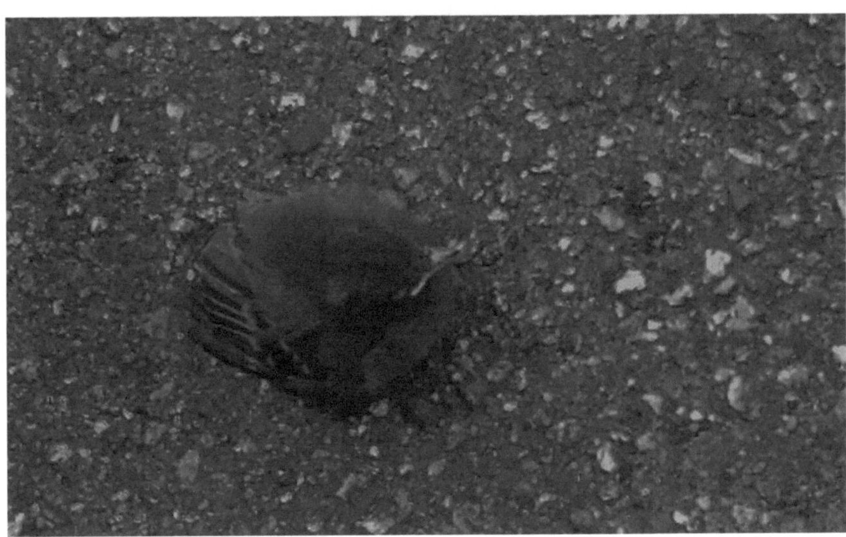

Mother, I wanted to give you a gift,
But I have no money, only these broken shells
From where the loon carried her necklace.
In the old story she received her necklace
From shells thrown around the loon's neck and set in place,
And now there is only pain, the necklace torn off.

And did you walk, my Boy,

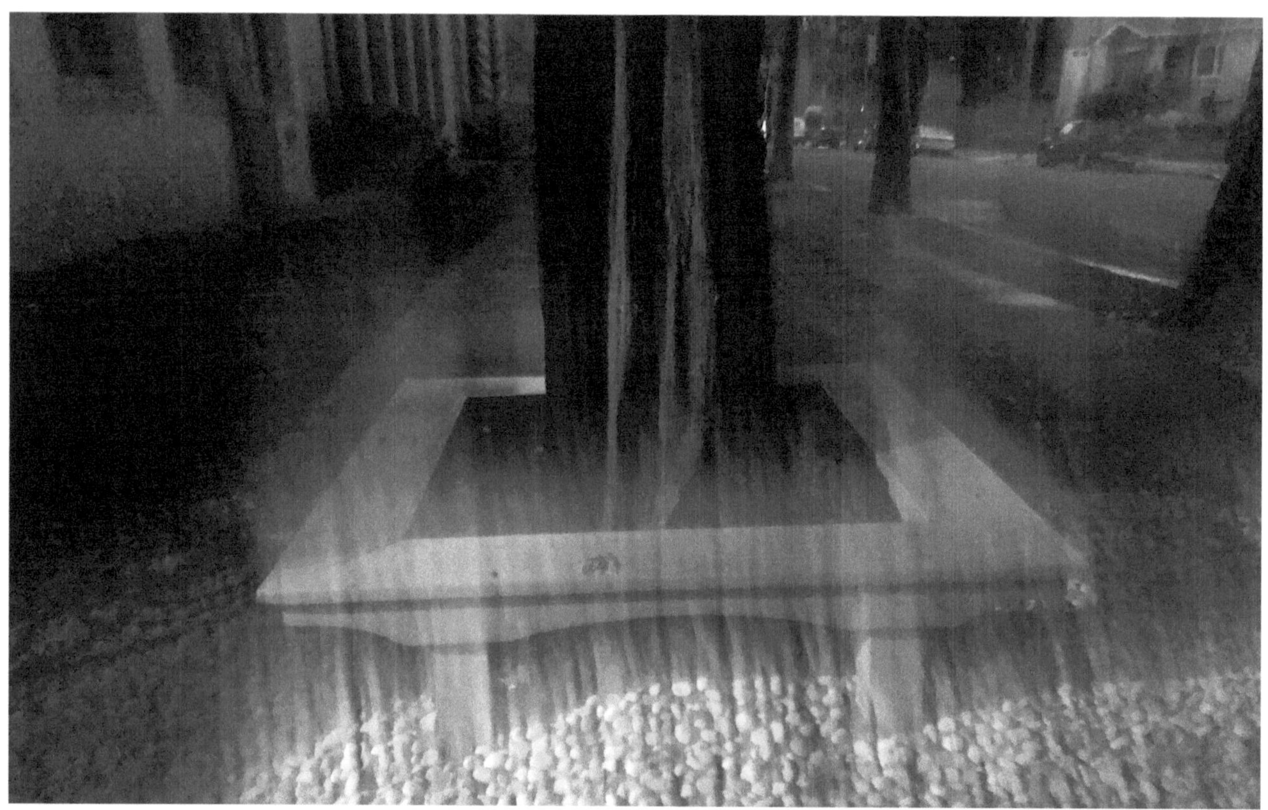

between the rows of trees?

# The Short Day's Dark

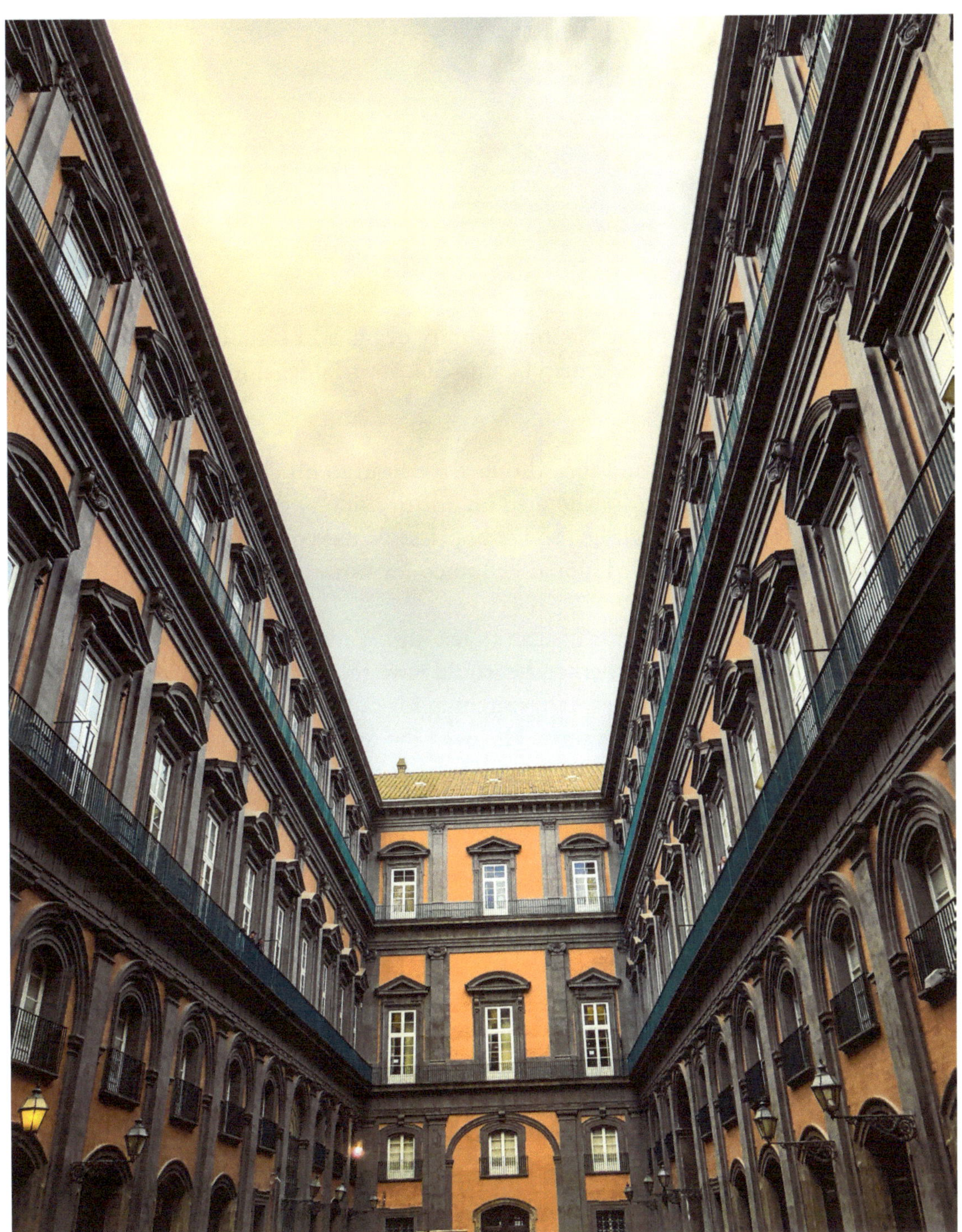

Marco's
Tears on the glass
Covering autographs
Of Leopardi in Naples
In mind.

"Scusatemi, Signori," said the archivist in the National Library of Italia in Napoli, "Excuse me, I must close the lid to protect these priceless papers of our esteemed Count Giacomo Taldegardo Francesco di Sales Saverio Pietro Leopardi."

Marco looked at me as he began to weep and then dropped his head to his chest, so moved that he could view up close the true hand of his poeta Leopardi, who died on one dry side of the vulcano Vesuvio centuries past, now gone. Marco looked into my eyes. I felt helpless… hopeless. What could I offer him, this vero Napolitano, a true Neapolitan? I caught him and steadied him as he leaned forward toward the case.

I was speechless. I, too, love Leopardi's poems: I began to tear up. We were in Napoli, home of dramatic gestures, and though Leopardi was born a Northerner, he would have recognized our gestures and, I believe, appreciated them… and perhaps seen us as poets, too, searching for our own words and paths. Leopardi lived a difficult life. And unfulfilled in multitudinous ways. He loved the moon deeply, but she did not replace an actual woman for him. That poor sad man wrote in "To the moon," as I have translated:

> And yet, recollecting
> and recounting the times of my grief
> comforts me.

Certainly I love the moon, too, and unrequited, surely, as I look back and forward in my little life, remembering an early fantastic love I created whole cloth out of young women:

> Just a kid, waiting for the fair to come,
> and then after it's gone, lying all tear-faced
> in my pillow; and then, late at night, I hear
> those lonely sounds going off and dying,
> bit-by-bit, my heart breaking the same as now.
> from my imitation of Giacomo Leopardi's
> "La sera del dì di festa"

In public, tears do help. I held Marco's shoulder with my hand, and together we cried. I felt freed to remember my own griefs and cry for them as well.

We love
Leopardi
As if Giacomo lived
Still on a hill or volcano
High up.

And then, standing in that special room, a memory flowed into my tears, flooding the moment with the faces of my parents, who'd both died in these past five years. For a beat I was entirely alone, as we all are when our parents have died. Then the calm voice of the young librarian brought me back: "Signore, siamo tutti pronti. Andiamo nella sala programmi per la lettura." Yes, I am ready for the reading, I thought, and followed her into the room nearby.

Educator and poeta Marco Rossi-Doria and his good friend Marco de Gemmis, an editore who has published me and also a poeta himself, were the reasons that I could look into these cases of Leopardi's hand writings here in Napoli. And on this auspicious visit thanks to their work, I had been invited by a fresh young librarian to read my poems and translations in an ongoing reading series at the National Library of Italia in Napoli. Grazie mille, amici! Along with my colleague and old friend artist/printer Robert Woods, I had brought along samples of our illustrated broadside work, some exhibiting my translations from the Italian, to show, display, and donate to the National Library of Italia in Napoli, a true mitzvah… from our press, Lines & Faces, and for us, an opportunity to give.

And in some important ways, I owe Rossi-Doria nearly everything: yes, he is generous and has demonstrated love for me and all my family. But it is much more than that. Marco's mother, Annie Lengyel, before she married Manlio Rossi-Doria, a revered agricultural economist in the Mezzogiorno, a war hero in the Resistance, jailed by Mussolini, and later a Senatore in Rome, had introduced my parents back in the early 1940s when they were all patriotic Communists together at UCLA, just before Dad shipped off to fight the fascists in WWII. Later was I made and possible!

And in that year I had lived in Napoli with my family, 1965-1966, Annie found our apartment, just below theirs on Via Posillipo. And also found  schools for my sister and me, my sister's the private Scuola Svizzera and mine the then-named public Liceo Tecnico e Comerciale E. di Nicola in the Vomero, the hilltop district, that looms over the center of Napoli below. And Annie was then a physical therapist and took good care of my injured back while Manlio and my Dad smoked Toscano cigars on their balcony. Of course, I had a secret crush on Marco's mother Annie, who wouldn't? Yes, her diamond-shaped face was beautiful, and she spoke all of her languages flawlessly—Hungarian, Italian, English. And certainly she spoke some German and French as well. Annie's strong fingers and warm hands managed my injury skillfully. When she was finished working my back, she stood and stretched her shoulders into her pretty, curly hair, and her chest pushed forward. Beautiful!

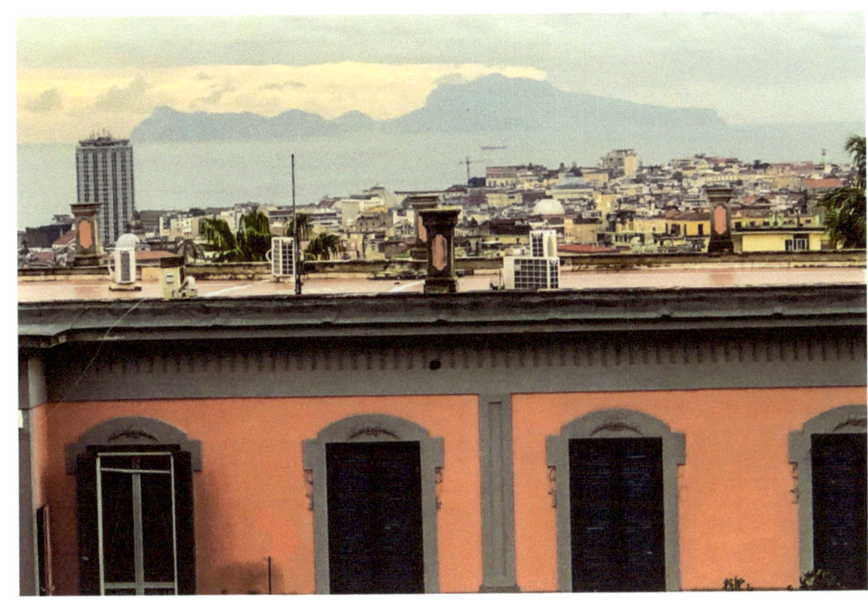

At the reading I presented some poems in English and some in Italian. The Marcos read much of the Italian, especially the originals from which I had translated. Rossi-Doria read all the Leopardi poems, but felt unequipped to read the Dante sestina, "Al poco giorno e al gran cerchio d'ombra," ("To the short day's dark and the vast ring of shadow") so de Gemmis read it flawlessly. I read my translation, worked up nearly fifty years ago under the tutelage of classicist Donald Carne-Ross at Boston University. As I read, I was moved more than I expected, the rhythms of a stony journey toward a lovely woman never quite accomplished. The audience was especially appreciative of this translation. All seemed to know the poem. After I finished reading it, I looked out the window into the early evening in late Fall as it darkened our vulcano Vesuvio, the short day's dark, "Al poco giorno e al gran cerchio d'ombra."

**Dante Alighieri, Giacomo Leopardi, and Marco Rossi-Doria**

**ve voglio bene assaje**
**I wish you all well**

from Rime per la donna pietra by Dante Alighieri:
Al poco giorno e al gran cerchio d'ombra

Toward the short day's dark and the vast ring of shadow
I've come sadly, and to the whitening of the hills,
there where my eyes can find no color in the grass:
and yet, my longing remains evergreen,
it is fast-rooted so in the hard stone
which speaks and hears as if it were a woman.

In like fashion this ever-new woman
remains as hard as snow within a shadow;
for she is not moved any more than stone
by the sweet season that warms the foothills,
and returns them from white to April green,
bringing a cover of flowers and of grass.

When in her hair she's set a garland of grass,
she keeps from every mind every other woman;
for in the mix, crisping yellow and the green
are so lovely, Love seeks out their shadow,
Love who has locked me in among the low hills
more tightly than hardened mortar padlocks stone.

Her beauty has more power than a rare stone,
and she gives wounds that cannot be healed by grass;
for this I've fled over plains and over hills,
to venture an escape from such a woman;
but from her light I cannot find a shadow,
under knoll or wall or in the forest-green.

Just now I saw her dressed in the finest green,
so fair she would have instilled in a stone
the love I have even for her shadow;
so I have wanted her in a fresh field of grass
as much in love as ever was any woman,
and closed in all around by the highest hills.

But well may rivers return to the hills,
before flames catch in this wood, so wet and green,
as flame would catch in the heart of a fine woman
for me; I who would sleep willingly on stone
all my days and wander feeding on grass,
if only to see where her dress casts shadow.

Whenever the hills cast the blackest shadow,
Under summer-green this fair young woman
hides it, as a man hides a stone in the grass.

– Dante Alighieri
translated by Alan Bern

https://static1.squarespace.com/static/578bbb8bb8a79bbf14deccd7/t/57962e-9037c58136e65ecd52/1469460115905/sestina2.jpg

Al poco giorno e al gran cerchio d'ombra
son giunto, lasso!, ed al bianchir de' colli,
quando si perde lo color ne l'erba;
e 'l mio disio però non cangia il verde,
si è barbato ne la dura petra
che parla e sente come fosse donna.

Similemente questa nova donna
si sta gelata come neve a l'ombra;
che non la move, se non come petra,
il dolce tempo che riscalda i colli
e che li fa tornar di bianco in verde
perché li copre di fioretti e d'erba.

Quand'ella ha in testa una ghirlanda d'erba,
trae de la mente nostra ogn'altra donna;
perché si mischia il crespo giallo e 'l verde
sì bel, ch'Amor lì viene a stare a l'ombra,
che m'ha serrato intra piccioli colli
più forte assai che la calcina petra.

La sua bellezza ha più vertù che petra,
e 'l colpo suo non può sanar per erba;
ch'io son fuggito per piani e per colli,
per potere scampar da cotal donna;
e dal suo lume non mi può far ombra
poggio né muro mai né fronda verde.

Io l'ho veduta già vestita a verde
sì fatta, ch'ella avrebbe messo in petra
l'amor ch'io porto pur a la sua ombra;
ond'io l'ho chesta in un bel prato d'erba
innamorata, com'anco fu donna,
e chiuso intorno d'altissimi colli.

Ma ben ritorneranno i fiumi a' colli
prima che questo legno molle e verde
s'infiammi, come suol far bella donna,
di me; che mi torrei dormire in petra
tutto il mio tempo e gir pascendo l'erba,
sol per veder do' suoi panni fanno ombra.

Quandunque i colli fanno più nera ombra,
sotto un bel verde la giovane donna
la fa sparer, com'uom petra sott'erba.

—Dante Alighieri

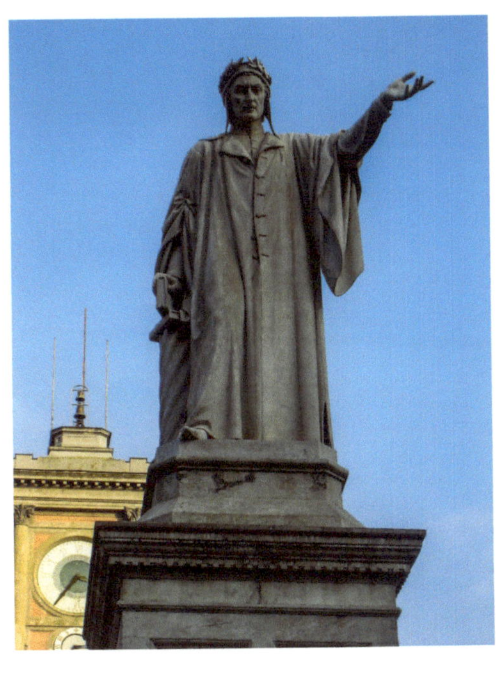

**O Dante**

Alighieri, I wish that you and Woods and I
could be taken up clearly into air
in a brilliant ship magically flying
and that in that sky we could go anywhere
we wanted without storm or turbulence
in any way facing our high flight,
but instead, that sharing all our thoughts,
we would want to stay together throughout the night.

And that the fair seer would bring us
Beatrice, Alice, and the lovely one
who lives at number thirty not far from us,
and speaking of sweet love all day long,
I know each of them would be as happy as
I believe that we would be, all three of us.

— Alan Bern's Imitation of Dante's "Guido, i' vorrei che tu e Lapo ed io"

Alighieri, I wish that you and Woods and I
could be taken up clearly into air
in a brilliant ship magically flying
and that in that sky we could go anywhere
we wanted without storm or turbulence
in any way facing our high flight,
but instead, that sharing all our thoughts,
we would want to stay together throughout the night.
And that the fair seer would bring us
Beatrice, Alice, and the lovely one
who lives at number thirty not far from us,
and speaking of sweet love all day long,
I know each of them would be as happy as
I believe that we would be, all three of us.

— Alan Bern's Imitation of Dante's
"Guido, i'vorrei che tu e Lapo ed io"

Guido, i' vorrei che tu e Lapo ed io
fossimo presi per incantamento,
e messi in un vasel ch'ad ogni vento
per mare andasse al voler vostro e mio.
Sì che fortuna od altro tempo rio
non ci potesse dare impedimento,
anzi, vivendo sempre in un talento,
di stare insieme crescesse 'l disio.
E monna Vanna e monna Lagia poi
con quella ch'è sul numer de le trenta
con noi ponesse il buono incantatore:
e quivi ragionar sempre d'amore,
e ciascuna di lor fosse contenta,
sì come i' credo che saremmo noi.

— Dante Alighieri

**Infinitudes**

Zeno's thought
Leopardi's hill

A thick child's finger measures

the endless lines between the hatches

on the wood rule, dizzy

from counting in another language.

Later, shorn sheep

jumped the trimmed hedge,

landing back, lambs again,

pranced off on a measured track

toward a deeply colored sun,

rising or falling, dark

enclosing the child like a lid.

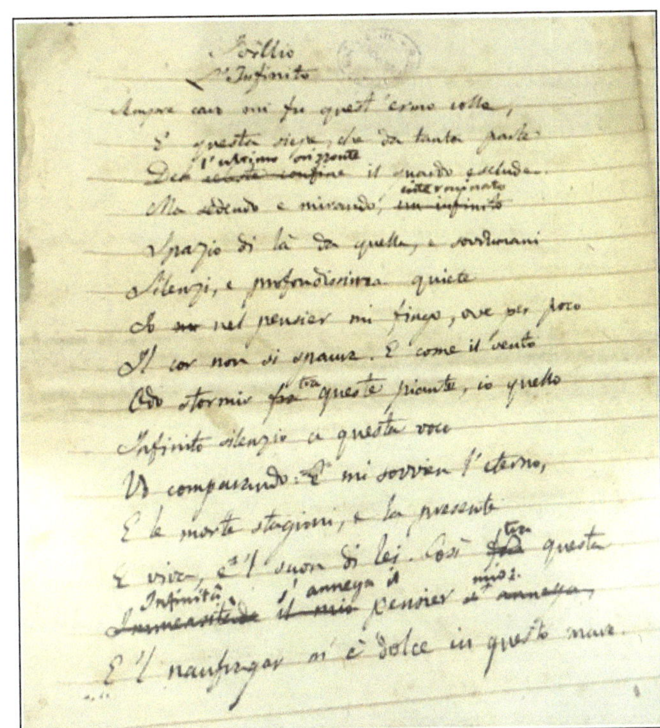

Idillio
L'Infinito
Sempre caro mi fu quest'ermo colle,
E questa siepe, che da tanta parte
Dell'ultimo orizzonte il guardo esclude.
Ma sedendo e mirando, interminati
Spazio di là da quella, e sovrumani
Silenzi, e profondissima quiete
Io nel pensier mi fingo, ove per poco
Il cor non si spaura. E come il vento
Odo stormir tra queste piante, io quello
Infinito silenzio a questa voce
Vo comparando: e mi sovvien l'eterno,
E le morte stagioni, e la presente
E viva, e 'l suon di lei. Così tra questa
Infinità s'annega il pensier mio:
E 'l naufragar m'è dolce in questo mare.

**The Infinite**

Always dear to me this solitary hil

and this thicket that screens out so much

of the view of the farthest horizon.

But sitting and gazing out, I frame in my mind

endless spaces beyond and silences that

surpass anything human, and a deep stiliness:

there for a single beat the heart is not afraid.

And as the wind comes murmuring among these

plants,

I begin to compare that infinite silence

to this voice: and I recollect eternity

and the dead seasons past and the present

one alive before me, and her sound. So in this

immensity my thinking goes under and sinks

and this ship going down is sweet to me in this sea.

Translated into English by Alan Bern
"L'infinto" by Giacomo Leopardi
In public domain

## The Infinite

Always dear to me this solitary hill
and this thicket that screens out so much
of the view of the farthest horizon.
But sitting and gazing out, I frame in my mind
endless spaces beyond and silences that
surpass anything human, and a deep stillness;
there for a single beat the heart is not afraid.
And as the wind comes murmuring among these plants,
I begin to compare that infinite silence
to this voice: and I recollect eternity
and the dead seasons past and the present
one alive before me, and her sound. So in this
immensity my thinking goes under and sinks
and this ship going down is sweet to me in this sea.

— Giacomo Leopardi
translated by Alan Bern

## L'infinito

Sempre caro mi fu quest'ermo colle,
e questa siepe, che da tanta parte
dell'ultimo orizzonte il guardo esclude.
Ma sedendo e mirando, interminati
spazi di là da quella, e sovrumani
silenzi, e profondissima quïete
io nel pensier mi fingo, ove per poco
il cor non si spaura. E come il vento
odo stormir tra queste piante, io quello
infinito silenzio a questa voce
vo comparando: e mi sovvien l'eterno,
e le morte stagioni, e la presente
e viva, e il suon di lei. Così tra questa
immensità s'annega il pensier mio:
e il naufragar m'è dolce in questo mare.

— Giacomo Leopardi

## Make hay while the sun shines

The young thing's comin' in from the country
with the sun near-set,
carrying her sack of grass,
and her all set
to get decked out with roses and violets –
in her hair and 'round her neck –
like always, cause tomorrow's Sunday.
Grannie's sittin'
in the dyin' sun,
spinnin', talkin' to the ladies,
rememb'ring the days that used to be
when they all dressed up
to dance the night away –
they were fresh and quick back then,
and so were the young pups who chased 'em.
Dusk again: the land's as brown as a bear;
and the sky's fulla light, blue air:
the shadows fall from the hills and roof-tops
in the light of the white, new moon comin' up.
I hear church bells ringin'
the holiday in.
You might call it a heart-comfortin' sound.
The kids leave down the wash and the wood,
splash 'round and around
in the coolin' stream, frolickin' under the bridge,
jumpin' like crickets do,
happy as larks they sound.
The farmhand whistles
on his way home, thinks to himself
tomorrow he won't work for nothin',
'cause tomorrow's restful Sunday.

Then everythin' 'comes quiet,

the lights are out.
I hear a rasp filin' away
and a hammer thumpin' – say,
the carpenter's workin' all night
by lanternlight: in his locked-up shop
he rushes to finish the job
before dawn 'rouses up the town.

From the old seven-shooter
this is the best-hearted day,
fulla hopes and joys:
tomorrow in the thought
of the work-a-day life comin' up,
you'll wish that tiresome, gloomy day'd stop.

Young whippersnapper, boy! yours is the bloomin' age,
like this whole-happy day,
this clear and hold-your-breath Saturday
'waits tomorrow's holiday
of your life. Live it full, child,
this is the gladdest time, what the old codger called
'the sweet-tempered season.'
That's all I'm sayin': just don't let it worry you
if tomorrow's slow comin'.

— Inspiration from Robert Lowell's
Imitation of Giacomo Leopardi's
"Il sabato del villaggio"
by Alan Bern

## Il Sabato del villaggio

La donzelletta vien dalla campagna,
In sul calar del sole,
Col suo fascio dell'erba; e reca in mano
Un mazzolin di rose e di viole,
Onde, siccome suole,
Ornare ella si appresta
Dimani, al dì di festa, il petto e il crine.
Siede con le vicine
Su la scala a filar la vecchierella,
Incontro là dove si perde il giorno;
E novellando vien del suo buon tempo,
Quando ai dì della festa ella si ornava,
Ed ancor sana e snella
Solea danzar la sera intra di quei
Ch'ebbe compagni dell'età più bella
Già tutta l'aria imbruna,
Torna azzurro il sereno, e tornan l'ombre
Giù da' colli e da' tetti,
Al biancheggiar della recente luna.
Or la squilla dà segno
Della festa che viene;
Ed a quel suon diresti
Che il cor si riconforta.
I fanciulli gridando
Su la piazzuola in frotta,
E qua e là saltando,
Fanno un lieto romore:
E intanto riede alla sua parca mensa,
Fischiando, il zappatore,
E seco pensa al dì del suo riposo
Poi quando intorno è spenta ogni altra face,
E tutto l'altro tace,
Odi il martel picchiare, odi la sega
Del legnaiuol, che veglia

Nella chiusa bottega alla lucerna,
E s'affretta, e s'adopra
Di fornir l'opra anzi il chiarir dell'alba.
Questo di sette è il più gradito giorno,
Pien di speme e di gioia:
Diman tristezza e noia
Recheran l'ore, ed al travaglio usato
Ciascuno in suo pensier farà ritorno.
Garzoncello scherzoso,
Cotesta età fiorita
È come un giorno d'allegrezza pieno,
Giorno chiaro, sereno,
Che precorre alla festa di tua vita.
Godi, fanciullo mio; stato soave,
Stagion lieta è cotesta.
Altro dirti non vo'; ma la tua festa
Ch'anco tardi a venir non ti sia grave.

— Giacomo Leopardi

## To Himself

Now you will be at rest
forever, weary heart of mine, for it has perished,
that final deceiver, the one I believed eternal. Perished. Well
aware, of the deceptions dear to us,
not just the hope, the desire is dead.
Rest forever. You have beaten
enough. Not worth anything to anyone
your beating, neither is earth worthy
of sighs. Bitter and boring
is life, nothing else; and the world is sludge.
Calm yourself now. Despair
for the final time. To our humankind fate
has given only death. Now despise
yourself, nature, the brute
power that reigns undercover damaging all of us,
and the infinite vanity of all things.

— Giacomo Leopardi
translated by Alan Bern

## A se stesso

Or poserai per sempre,
stanco mio cor. Perí l'inganno estremo,
ch'eterno io mi credei. Perí. Ben sento,
in noi di cari inganni,
non che la speme, il desiderio è spento.
Posa per sempre. Assai
palpitasti. Non val cosa nessuna
i moti tuoi, né di sospiri è degna
la terra. Amaro e noia
la vita, altro mai nulla; e fango è il mondo.
T'acqueta omai. Dispera
l'ultima volta. Al gener nostro il fato
non donò che il morire. Omai disprezza
te, la natura, il brutto
poter che, ascoso, a comun danno impera,
e l'infinita vanità del tutto.

— Giacomo Leopardi

## To the moon

Oh moon, beauteous moon, I remember now
that as the days count down a year, up, up this hill
I came, in my misery, to gaze at you again:
and you hung over those woods then,
as you do now, brightening everything.
But tears came and spilled over my lashes
blurring your face and making it flicker
in my open eyes, so tormented I was
in my life, and am still, the way does not change,
oh my dearest moon. And yet, recollecting
and recounting the times of my grief
comforts me. Oh, how pleasant is the pain
in youthful times, when hope has such a long stretch
ahead and memory such a short span,
the remembrance of things past, although sad,
and though the agony will endure!

— Giacomo Leopardi
translated by Alan Bern

## Alla luna

O graziosa luna, io mi rammento
che, or volge l'anno, sovra questo colle
io venia pien d'angoscia a rimirarti:
e tu pendevi allor su quella selva
siccome or fai, che tutta la rischiari.
Ma nebuloso e tremulo dal pianto
che mi sorgea sul ciglio, alle mie luci
il tuo volto apparia, che travagliosa
era mia vita: ed è, né cangia stile,
o mia diletta luna. E pur mi giova
la ricordanza, e il noverar l'etate
del mio dolore. Oh come grato occorre
nel tempo giovanil, quando ancor lungo
la speme e breve ha la memoria il corso,
il rimembrar delle passate cose,
ancor che triste, e che l'affanno duri!

— Giacomo Leopardi

## AS A DEDICATION

To you
you with the jet-black hair
watching for my caresses
down your back,
jet-black eyes.

—Translated into English by Alan Bern
"COME UNA DEDICA" by Marco Rossi-Doria

## COME UNA DEDICA

A te
capelli neri
che spiano le mie carezze
lungo la schiena tua,
occhi neri.

—Marco Rossi-Doria

## I'VE TOLD YOU

I've told you
I've told you:
the husbands were captured
by ambitions, by scams
and the wives I don't know.

The daughters though
they came to ask
about this house so full of light
left just like this.

— Translated into English by Alan Bern
"TE L'HO DETTO" by Marco Rossi-Doria

## TE L'HO DETTO

Te l'ho detto
te l'ho detto
i mariti furono presi
da ambizioni da raggiri
e le mogli io non lo so.
Le figlie però
vennero a chiedere
di questa casa pieno di luce
lasciata così.

— Marco Rossi-Doria

## Michelangelo Merisi da Caravaggio's

"The Seven Works of Mercy"
after Neapolitan Mass
Caravaggio's The Seven Works of Mercy

American pennies
here and there in sidewalk puddles
in front of the Duomo,
la Cattedrale di San Gennaro,
a black man and a small pale woman
at far grey columns
both wrapped in rags, hold knees close

Around the corner
understanding only some of
the words of the Mass
at Pio Monte
della Misericordia
seats between the Few
hearing the young priest
speaking in crisp words
a Beatrice enters
at the last prayer
standing, her head hung
all of us under
Caravaggio's

grand Le Opere
di Misericordia
from dark deepnesses
faces, hands, a single breast feeds
a very old man, her papà,
head over a prison stone
not a here-and-there
swirling suffering

ascends through an Angel's wing
descends through a Nobleman
about to clothe the naked
bright white back of he
whose left hand holds this whole world
from tile up and out into
the richest darkness
imaginable
seen also in day
as in the late night
the most poor shaking alone
in front of the Cathedral
closing for the day
into moonless nightquiet
cold growing always colder

hovering CODA: Yes, there is a true cross
Structuring the work
With lower figures leaning
Away from the dark
Central vertical
The horizontal
At an angle curving off

In the upper left
Grey Neapolitan drapes,
Or perhaps laundry,
On one side, on the other
The dark space between
One Angel's grey wings
Yes, the same grey shade

This Angel's arms
Embraces another Angel
Both fly into the painting
Back into the warm darkness

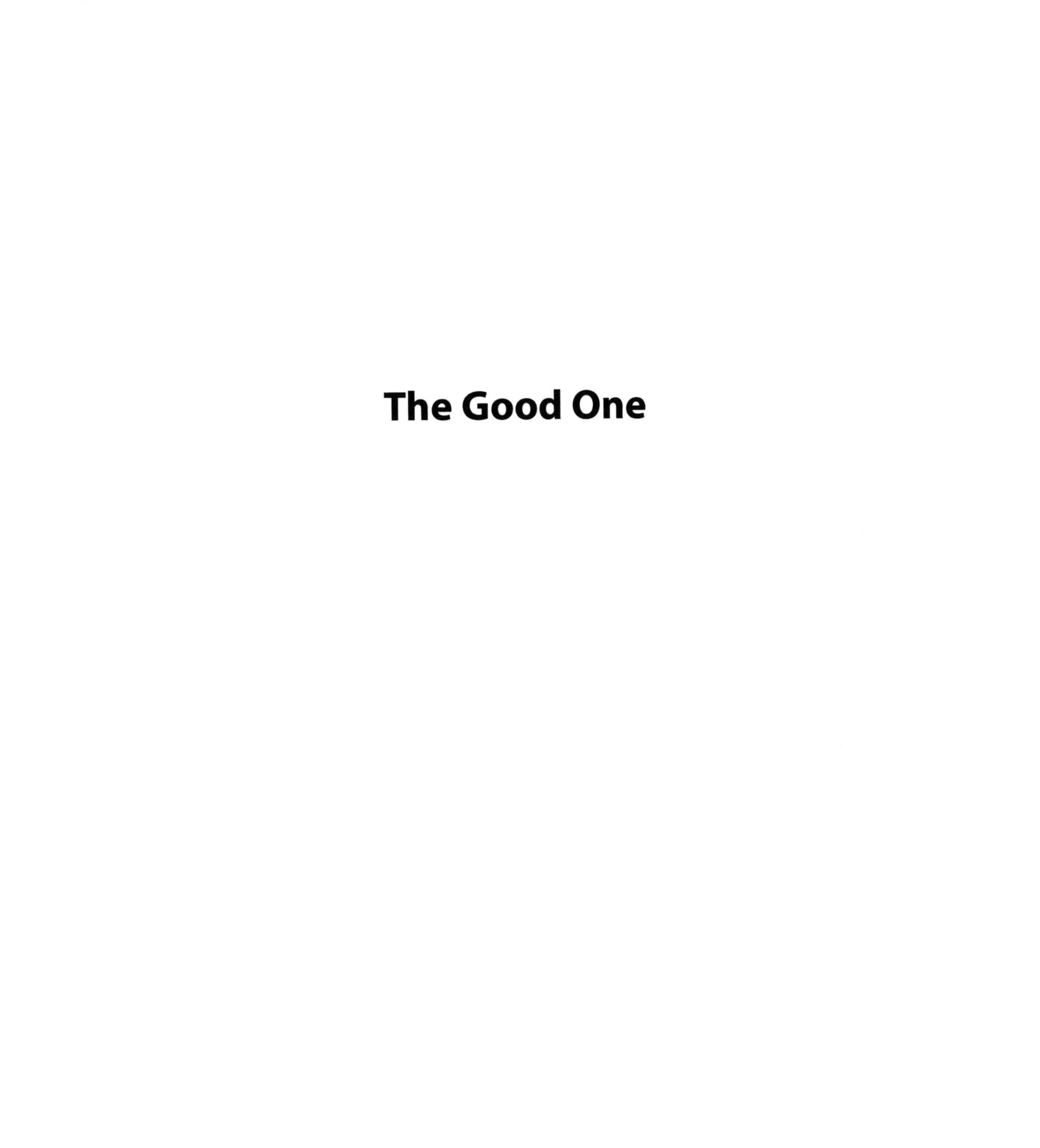

# The Good One

# The Good One

My Neapolitan friend Marco and I had time to walk a bit after lunch, to let the rich food settle, as the Italian's call this time "nel dopo pranzo." We walked into one of the poorest parts of Napoli, I Quartieri Spagnoli (the Spanish Quarters), so named because this section once housed the Spanish soldiers who accompanied such luminaries as the Portuguese-born Jewish statesman, advisor to Kings, philosopher, Bible commentator, and financier—and remarkable ancestor of my wife Alice—the great Don Isaac Abravanel (often called by scholars, "The Abrabanel") after he was banished from Spain because of the Inquisition.

I told Marco about Don Isaac, and he asked me what happened to Don Isaac after his banishment. I continued as we walked: "At the time of his banishment, Toledo was Don Isaac's home—he came to Napoli travelling through Genova along with his brethren and sistren, and he lived there for a time in peace until the French took over Napoli and he left to go south to Sicilia. Eventually Don Isaac went to Venezia, but when he died there, he had to be taken to Padova to be buried since no burials were allowed for Jews in Venezia at that time. The bottom line, I explained to Marco, is that Don Isaac was a Jew and lived for a time next door to your apartment building. And I'm a Jew, my wife is a Jew, and, of course, Marco, you are a Jew as well."

I Quartieri Spagnoli include a section called Montecalvario (Mount of Calvary), named for the 16th century complex of churches of that name. On our digestive walk, Marco, in typical fashion, asked as he rat-a-tat told me about Sacri Monti (Sacred Mounts): "What makes these Sacri Monti in the Piemonte so special? They are everywhere! We have them here in Napoli, right here in Montecalvario. Look!" He spoke as he pointed at little altars, many of them eye-high and sitting in the walls along our walk back from our lunch of Pasta alla Genovese, which is, by the way, a Neapolitan dish, based perhaps, in part, on some potato-related thoughts (even though onions are its base) from Genova—or, perhaps, invented by someone called Genovese. I had some pedantic answers to his questions, but mostly kept quiet. In fact, everywhere does have its version of altezza, or heights, its holy hills, its emblems of the suffering of our human journey, or a Via Crucis, and its various story-stations, its Sacri Monti chapels. And rest assured this is, by no means, a purely Catholic phenomenon—so say we Jews, both Marco, religious, and I, secular.

As we turned the corner to go up a stairway, which would take us to his vicolo, his little street, and to his apartment where we could have an afternoon nap, we saw a large crowd surrounding a police car that blocked our way. Several of those who milled, smoked and smoked. Several other young men and women were talking loudly to two very tired-looking policemen. Something was not right here. Marco went directly over to one of the smokers, a young woman, and started talking in dialect, fast very fast. Everyone seems to know Marco in Montecalvario, perhaps because he has helped so many of them or their children (to escape drug addiction, to finish school while carrying a baby to term, to find the right kind of job, whether they've graduated or not, a job that can sustain over the longer term)— Marco is known in some educational circles as il maestro di strada, the teacher in the streets. In Montecalvario, Marco is, absolutely, the professore even when he has worked in the country's Department of Education. Some treat him as if he were Mayor of I Quartieri Spagnoli.

Marco's hands were moving and his bald head bobbing. He had become pretty excited, too. It turned out that an old woman who owned a building next to where the police car was sitting had made a complaint to the police to have an altar removed from her property. I asked why. There are altars all over Montecalvario, I thought: they are the Sacri Monti chapels, the stations that tell the stories that Marco was just talking about.

Then, Marco told me this story: this altar was dedicated to a young man who had been accidentally killed by a young woman— they did not know each other— who on New Year's Eve 2008 had demanded from her boyfriend that he loan her his gun so that she could fire it off like fireworks at midnight. Crazy! I lived in Napoli in 1965; I recall that people threw everything out the window on New Year's Eve— garbage, old stuff they no longer wanted, pots of urine, even a baby or two. Horrifying! But a whole level different than firing a gun into the air in a crowded celebration. Wow! Totally insane! Che pazza!

This crowd was protesting the old woman's request. The altar contained merely a tabloid-sized painting made from a color photo of the young man, smiling, single
earring, and all. Who was he? I looked at his photo, and I felt very, very sad.

Marco went on that the young man's nickname was "o' Bono," Neapolitan dialect for "the good one." On New Year's Eve his mother had been nagging him to go out on the balcony to fetch back into the apartment his younger brother who was hanging out there, not a great place for a young kid to be. Yes, timing is everything, and the crazy young woman's shot had hit o' Bono just as he had gone out onto the balcony, killing him quickly.

In her gun ecstasy of New Year's, she had shot him dead. Then, quickly she had disappeared into I Quartieri Spagnoli for days, only to return and, then, turn herself in: "An accident, it was," she said.

Protests had started up. Not exactly against the young woman, but certainly against her behavior. A small self-organized group of young people from the Quartieri, some of them former students of Marco's, had gone to the authorities to ask for help, out of their difficult, poor lives, all for the good one, o' Bono, who had been himself quite disorganized, even lazy, never quite able to change his mode and behavior to finish school or hold a job. And, odd, and perhaps, worst of all, he had been a football fan of Juventus— and he living in Napoli!
He had been working on changing himself, bettering himself, but with little success.

Now never to be again. Never to be able to try again.

But they had all liked him, with all his foibles, for his sweetness, his goodness— even if he were a Juventus fan. And now he had been martyred. The group, in the name of Montecalvario, wanted help, help for themselves, help for their families, and help for their community. The authorities, predictably, had done little for them. The young woman has now been charged and will probably be found guilty of manslaughter.

The group had erected an altar, like so many other altars in Montecalvario, to remember. They would remember o' Bono, to recognize his worth. But now the police would take it down. No! In this odd, sad Calvario on a sacred, though often filthy, hill. And this, his chapel, his sacro monte, his last station, to remember him still.

Compromising perhaps, the police covered the altar with a plastic drape. At least o' Bono, the good one, might now be protected from the weather.

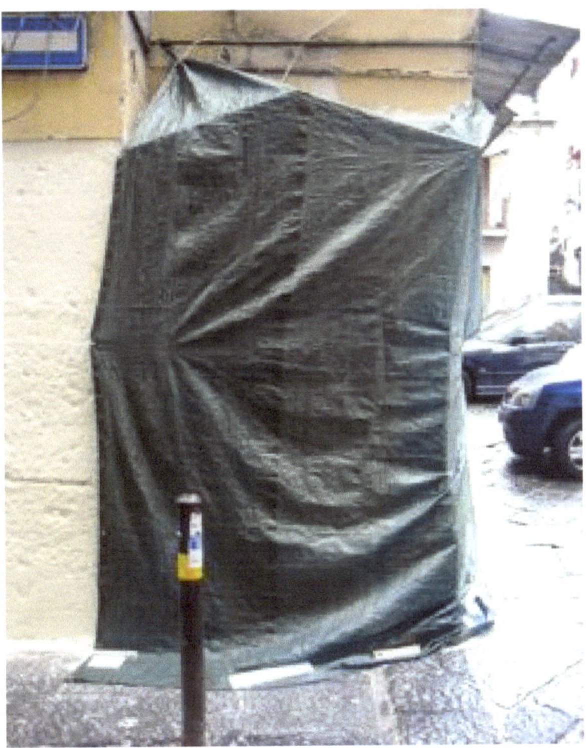

Sometimes the most important chapels
are completely masked by plastic.

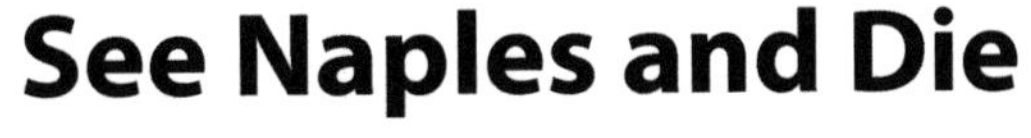

# See Naples and Die

# See Naples and Die

Vedi Napoli e poi muori

Marco, more pie, more pizza pie!
Stai 'nguaiato!
The oven's not even hot.
Ué!
Blessèd Mother, Gesù Cristo!
he's a know-nothing,
Well, he does have idioms,
and when the GI asks him
how he's doing,
he comes back with
tengo a uallera, thank you,
two long wallets
ready to rupture.
Sfaccim', he says
he has sperm in his hand towel,
and doesn't know
"whether" to put it.
What a fuckin' bother!
But in this mess
of traffic, here & there,
cars on every sidewalk,
he is a sprinting quail,
as the good Napolitani say
è 'nu brav' guaglion'!
a directed messenger
carrying fresh fish filets
wrapped tightly
in yesterday's news
and running
slapping both feet
a lit cigarette
on his lower lip

# See Naples and Die

Vedi Napoli e poi muori

Marco, ancora torta, ancora pizza pie![1]
Stai 'nguaiat[2]o!
Il forno neanche è caldo.
Ué!
Madre Benedetta, Gesù Cristo!
quello lì è un nonsaniente,
ma è ok?
Beh, lui gli idiomi ce li ha,
e quando il GI[3] gli chiede
come sta,
gli risponde svelto
tengo a uallera, thank you[4],
due scese bisacce
pronte a farsi ernia.
Sfaccim' dice lui
che c'ha lo sperma sull'asciuga-mano a tovaglietta,
e non sa
"se qualora" metterlo.
Che cazzo di fastidio!
Eppure in questo casino
di traffico di qua & di là,
macchine su ogni marciapiede,
lui è una quaglia zompettante,

---

1 Nel clima della poesia, nel miscuglio delle lingue da scoprire e che si scoprono, nell'evocazione di suoni e dell'immersione nelle parole della città da parte dell'autore allora adolescente qui viene usata la traduzione in American English degli anni sessanta della parola "pizza", che, allora, era "pizza pie", letteralmente "torta di pizza".
2 In Napoletano nel testo.
3 GI è il modo popolare per indicare dall'inizio del secolo scorso, in tutto il mondo, il soldato, aviere o marine delle forze armate degli stati Uniti. I soldati americani in città erano chiamati GI anche nei nostri quartieri dove giravano a centinaia dopo la guerra e fino a metà degli anni settanta, con la presenza del comando Nato Sud Europa a Napoli e la VI flotta ormeggiata nel golfo.
4 Questa strofa richiama il gioco di parole tra Inglese e Napoletano comunemente usato nell'inferenza tra ragazzini in mezzo alla strada e i GI: alla domanda "How are you?", si rispondeva "teng a uallera thank you".
In Napoletano nel testo.

come dicono i buon Napoletani
è 'nu brav' guaglion'[5]!
un messaggero comandato
che porta i filetti di fresco pesce
incartati stretti
nelle notizie di ieri
e che va correndo
come un matto dannato
per la sua preziosa vita.

— translated by Marco-Rossia Doria

5 In Napoletano nel testo.

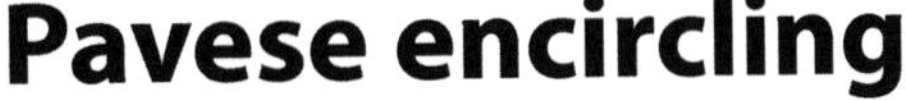

# Pavese encircling

# Pavese encircling

"Verrà la morte e avrà i tuoi occhi"
"Death will come and will have your eyes"

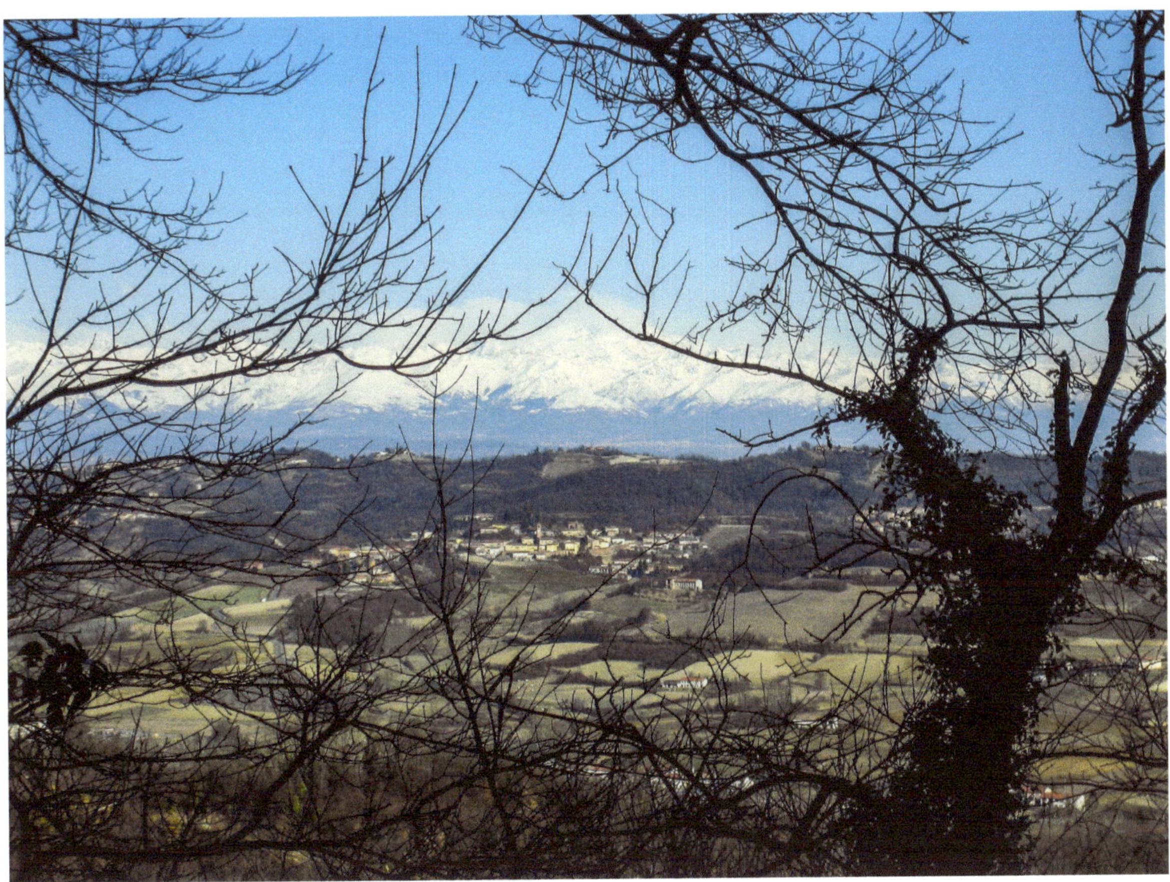

Late winter at the Sacro Monte of Crea. Winter visitors are few, the air fresh, often with a cold wind. The persistent, cheerful park guide explained that the great novelist, poet, and translator of American literature, Cesare Pavese, lived through part of World War II in the town just below, the Serralunga di Crea, self-exiled to avoid both fascist conscription and the difficult decision of joining the partisans. And depressed again, dumped again by a woman he loved. Solitudinous again.

What a powerful reminder: that Pavese spent time in this area. As I stepped along the edge-path and looked down, I thought of my own life and my times alone, sweet-and-sour together. My stop at Crea was one of the most happily isolated on my secular pilgrimage through the Sacri Monti of Northern Italia. And so memorable… probably because of my empathy for Pavese. Although never a Catholic nor a believer, I have often craved the quiet and the silence afforded to some of the religious in their cloistered lives. Knowing that Pavese had been there strengthened me in my own aloneness and surprised me, too. And although my hands felt cold, even in leather gloves, I was not bothered by the cold, so protected was I by the solemn resonance of that crisp air I breathed.

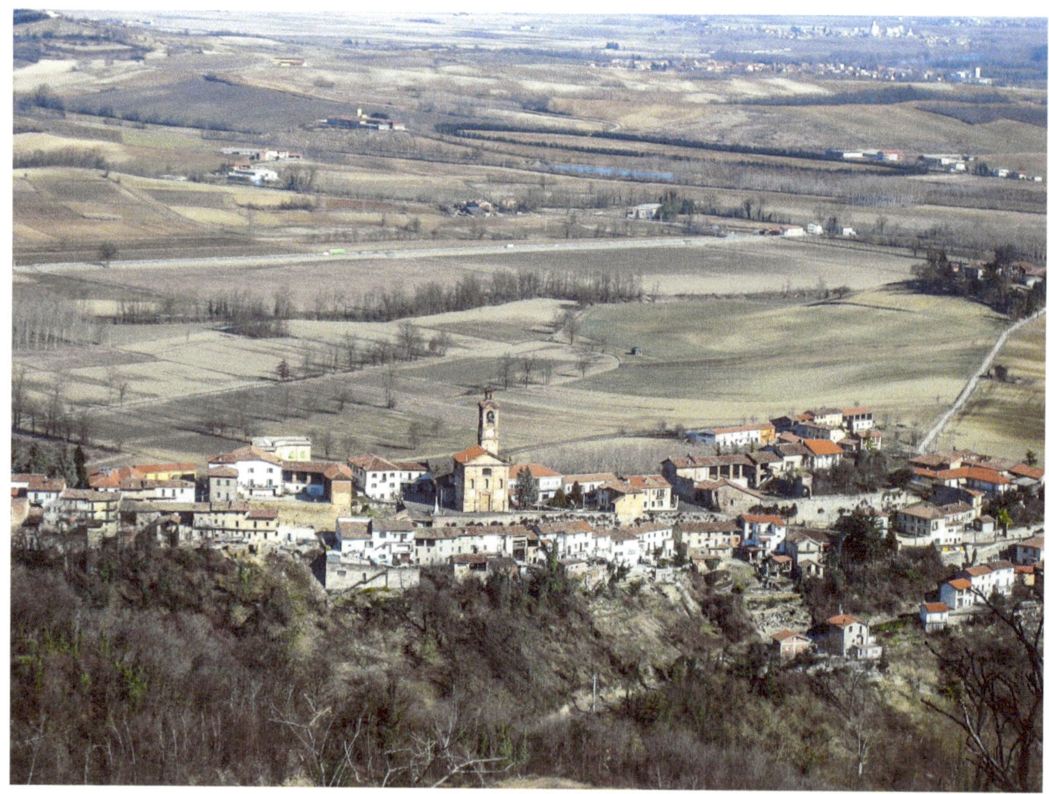

And I chose to have my morning caffè and eat my lunch in the meager Crea bar and buy minimal provisions there for my dinner as well. That way I could remain in the quiet of the Sacro Monte throughout the days and nights I was there.

Down below in the Serralunga di Crea, perhaps Pavese's asthma had been less cruel. And often he might have walked up the hillside – and, if so, certainly in mud, and, through the Sacro Monte, ever imagining America, her husky voice an ocean, and an ocean away.

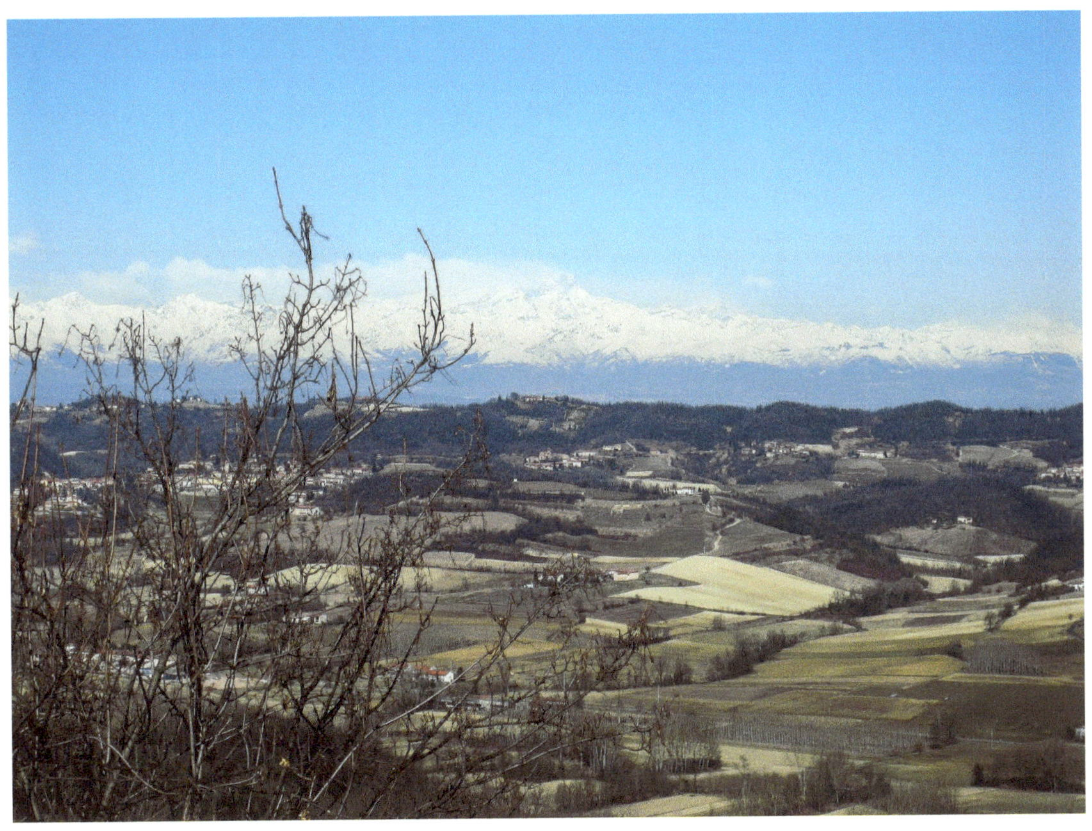

But would that have cheered him?
Walking can cheer.

I continued my walk along a path he might have used.

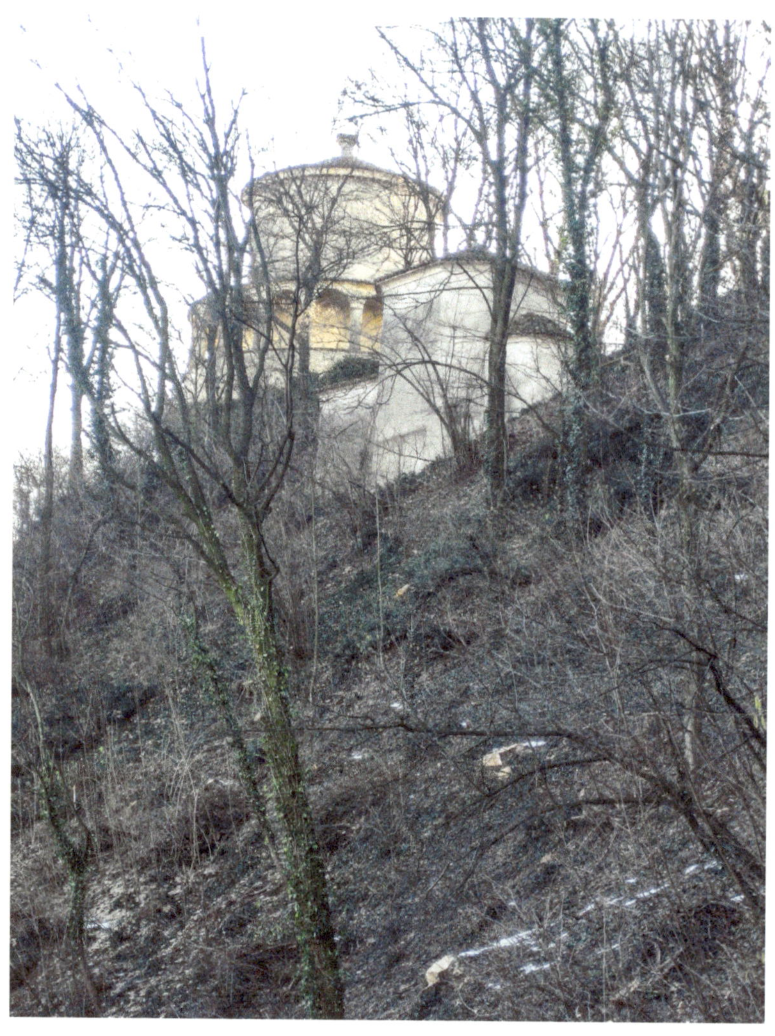

Perhaps he would have been cheered if he had reached the penultimate chapel. In the Sacri Monti of Italia are often found the stories of the lives of Jesus and Mary expressed with great passion, suffering, and theater, and ending in joy. Often one of the last chapels shows Paradise, and bears the name Il Paradiso.

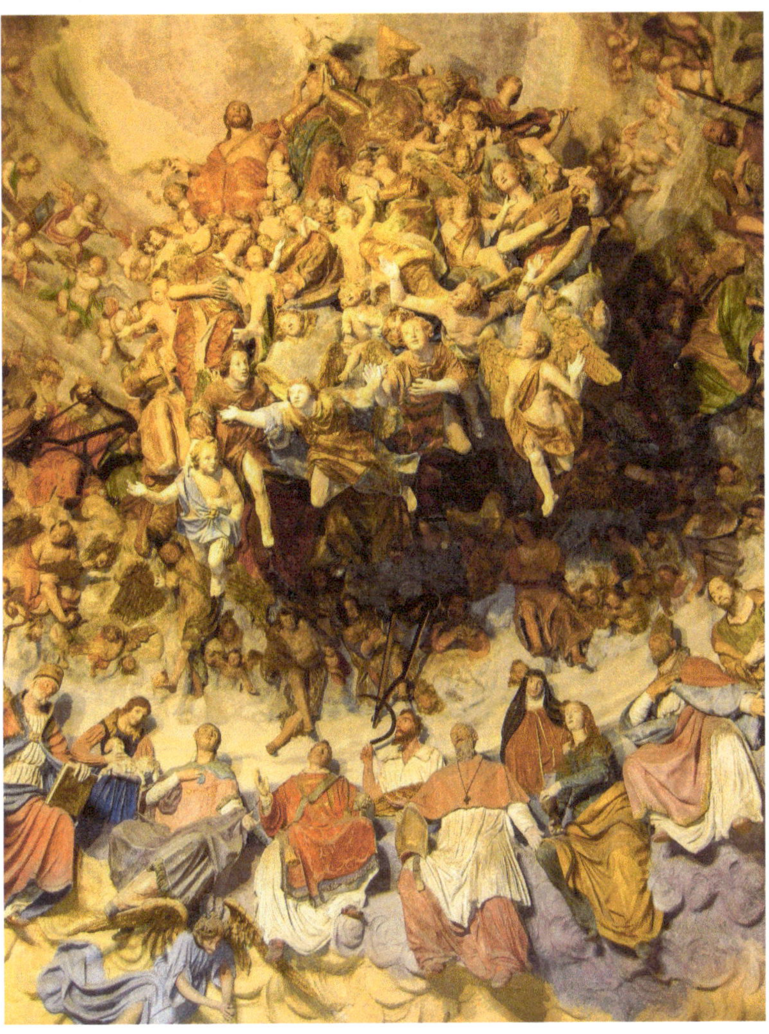

But this was Pavese: he might have favored the view out from the little covered terrace around the chapel. He might have circled, first clockwise, then turned and circled again, perhaps twice, counterclockwise.

Why did she leave me?

///

"Scenderemo nel gorgo muti."
"We shall descend into the gyre, mute."

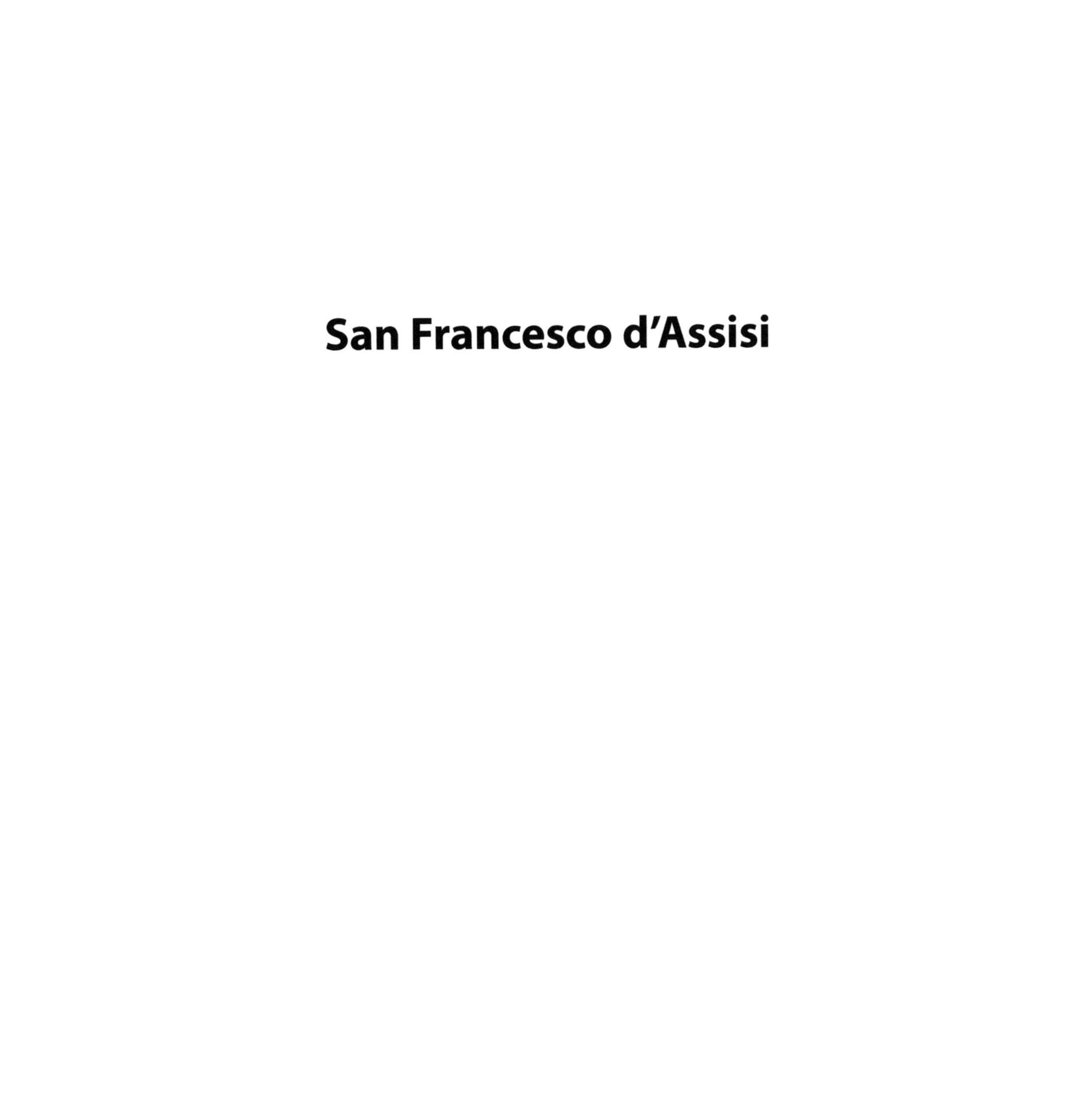

# San Francesco d'Assisi

## Final section of "Cantico di Frate Sole" or "Cantico delle Creature"

by San Francesco d'Assisi

Praised be for our Sister Mother Earth
who sustains and watches over us
and produces diverse fruits with colored flowers and with herbs.
Praised be for those who forgive with love
and for those who bear illness and tribulations.
Blessed be those who bear it all with patience
for they will be crowned with peace.
Praised be for our Sister of Bodily Death
from whom no one escapes alive:
troubles to those who die unreconciled;
blessed be those who die in sacred peace
for they will not be haunted, nor will they haunt.
Praises and blessings, all,
let us give thanks and serve each the other with respect
and with great humility.

Laudato si', mi' Signore, per sora nostra matre Terra,
la quale ne sustenta et governa,
et produce diversi fructi con coloriti flori et herba.
Laudato si', mi Signore, per quelli che perdonano per lo Tuo amore
et sostengono infirmitate et tribulatione.
Beati quelli ke 'l sosterranno in pace,
ka da Te, Altissimo, sirano incoronati.
Laudato si' mi Signore, per sora nostra Morte corporale,
da la quale nullu homo vivente po' skappare:
guai a quelli ke morrano ne le peccata mortali;
beati quelli ke trovarà ne le Tue sanctissime voluntati,
ka la morte secunda no 'l farrà male.
Laudate et benedicete mi signore,
et rengratiate et serviateli cun grande humilitate.

## Sacro Monte Above Orta

to San Francesco

At this Street
Sister Death, VIALE SORA MORTE,

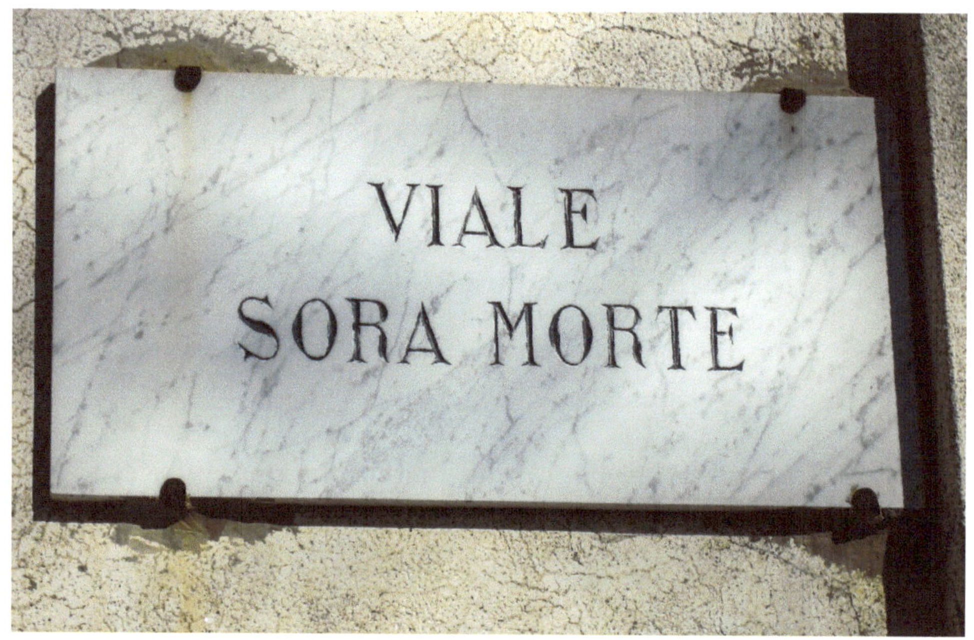


meet Sister Moon and Stars
Roundabout

A crescent bench watches meanderers

Behind me noon bells
across one valley

while its echoes forget
but do not forgive me

Sacred Mount, il Sacro Monte

turns with its curve
to peer across the lake,
il Lago d'Orta,
sun is a white tower, sky an impassable grey hill.

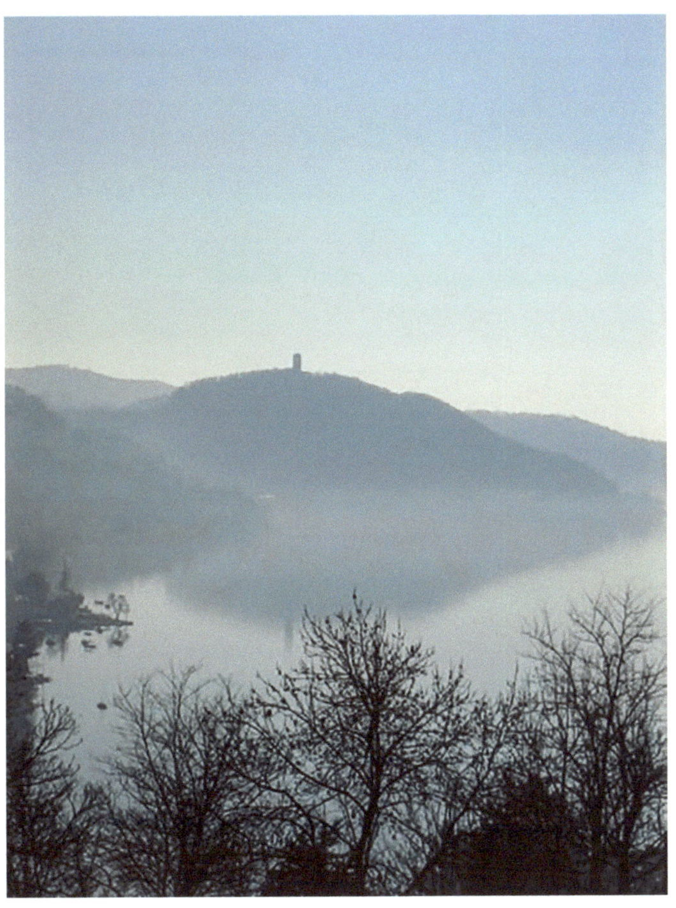

The air
 is where sound carries
hidden from every direction,

sun's bright sheer wall
glints down.
I am incised marble,
my own incisions unreadable
meet incised marble letters painted black:
ROTONDA SORA LUNA ET STELLE

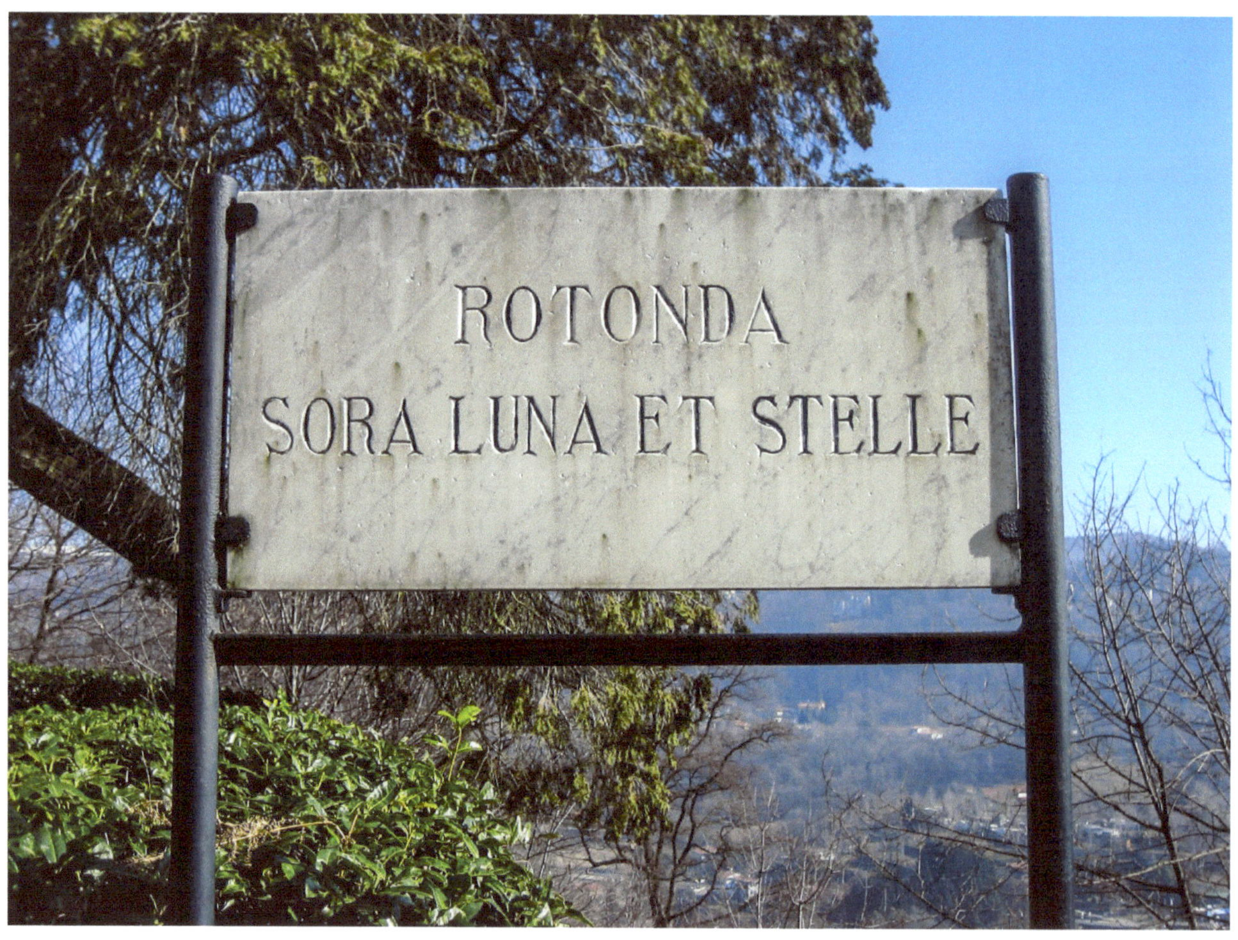


I will die here Sister Moon and Stars

will find nothing
to shadow in their light.

CODA:
I am still looking for  the slope of Memory Street,
VIALE RIMEMBRANZA,

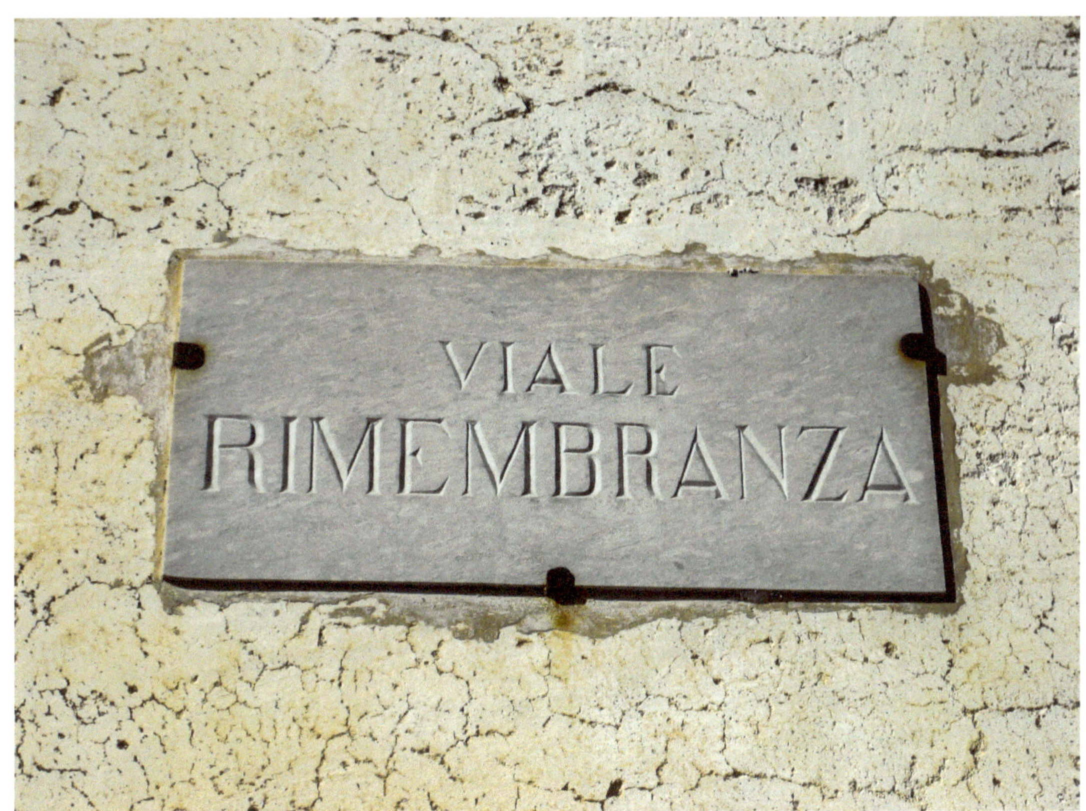


a street double-lined with tombs, named and dated.

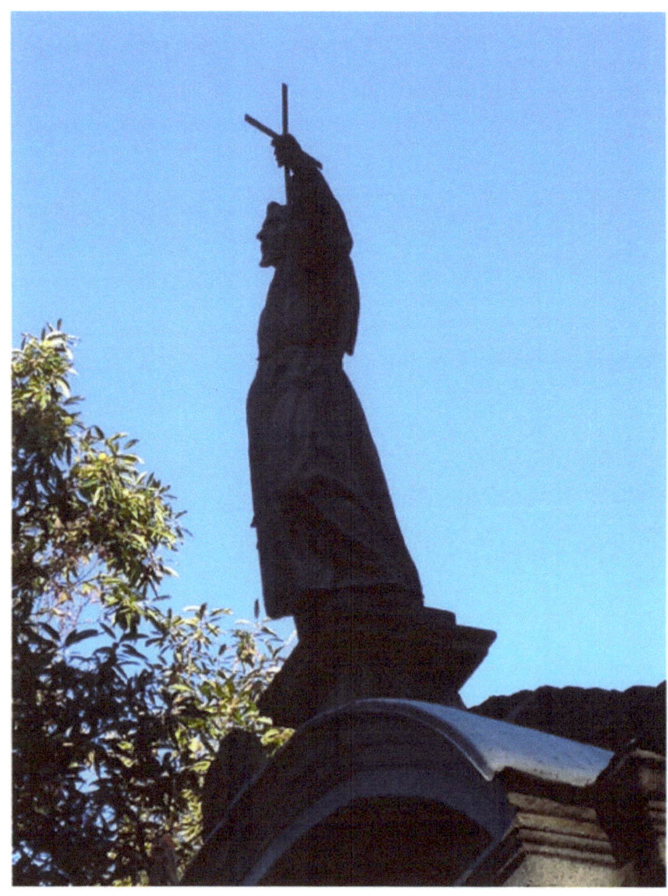

*Descent into Orta San Giulio*
*from the Sacro Monte di Orta*

Winter trees bide
they gate
Orta's Sacro Monte pathway,

branches, greened to pale bark,
lift death's face.

Lean Francesco, in stone, overlooks.

His stick-crucifix
held in cold air.

A first step it takes many
to sound out Francesco's words
chiseled at Chapel VI,

"go dear ones…announce peace and penance…
be patient…bless and thank everyone,"

just up Viale Frate Vento,
the Avenue of Brother Wind.

Though I falter in *penance*,
*peace* mumbled beyond me,

I walk back down a stony path
with loosened heart humming
*every*
*one*.

## Descent into Orta San Giulio

from the Sacro Monte di Orta

Winter trees bide

they gate

Orta's Sacro Monte pathway,

branches, bared to pale bark,

lift death's face.

Lean Francesco, in stone, overlooks.

His stick-crucifix

held in cold air.

A first step it takes many

to sound out Francesco's words

chiseled at Chapel VI,

"go dear ones…announce peace and penance…

be patient…bless and thank everyone,"

just up Viale Frate Vento,
the Avenue of Brother Wind.

Though I falter in penance,
peace mumbled beyond me,

I walk back down a stony path
with loosened heart humming
every
one.

## Hymn to San Francesco

who honored morning,
even the darkest hour of the wolf,
now I hear his birds begin,
and their songs mean light comes.
Here! I stretch over my scapula,
across the bed, and drive back down
to the dream I had in sleep.

## The Wolf of Gubbio

Francesco, holding the paw
of the great Wolf of Gubbio,
his nails sunk
deep into your palm.

This trust
attracted you
to pain
and the joy within it.

## IL LUPO DI GUBBIO

Francesco, tenendo la zampa
del grande Lupo di Gubbio,
i suoi artigli
affondarono profondi nel tuo palmo.

Questa fiducia
ti attirò
al dolore
e alla gioia che ha dentro.

— Translated by Marco-Rossi-Doria

## San Francesco

1315, Master of Saint Cecelia

San Francesco, you are so small,
head in a simple halo
hands pierced in prayer up
to Maria and her one son.
As a toddler, Gesú is a small adult
holding a colored bird
making a two-fingered sign
across her bosomy chest.

## from
## several stations in the Leggenda di San Francesco d'Assisi
## by Giotto di Bondone

the sky-hand of God
two-fingered sign to the raised
prayer hands of Francis

shall never forget
that moment and the poorman –
so my cape over the ground for him too
I cannot believe
that I exist without flames
running down my back

unless timepieces crack
the human father dies first
leaving the child
alone on a short porch looking
out over a rich, deep valley

though Francesco points
over his angry Father's head
Assisi now recalls
the Saint's parents in cold bronze,
broken chain in Mother's hands

green bird Francesco
fly up to your perch in air
uncaged throne of wood

this is what scared me most
the disappearance of my heart
and that no one knew the difference

## Assisi

Opened out, short at my feet,
I rise to find a desk height
tall enough to stand and lean.
I am completely naked
writing on this grocery bag
a list to take to market.
We need so many things.
Counting them on my fingers,
I drop the dull short pencil.
When I find it on my knees,
I raise my eyes and gasp out.
I am in the heaven of the sun,
and the only speech I give
croaks on: apples, onion, pear.

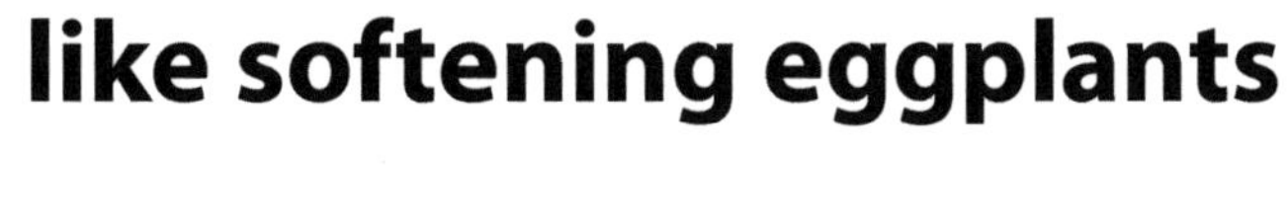

**like softening eggplants**

## a Nature

My biology teacher, Dad's first student Clyde, introduced me to nature through tasting and tonguing: treebark, leaves, dirts, small stones, even shed snakeskins and live bugs.

I remember
a late Summer afternoon
in Napoli
decades earlier
when I tasted Antonella—
delicious

## Dream of a green hillside

near you once more
before I go
and it is a close dance
the everlast
you are your
younger self
in a falling skirt
made of curtain
seen through
to your long softpants
beige corduroy smooth
at the waist
you are beautiful
as you move down the hill
lightly touch me kiss me
tell me you do still love me
as if it were true

## Your famous uncle

Zio Roberto wrote about
Fingering his wife
Side-watching her
In full blush

As he drove
Now their eyes straight ahead
While the kids
Napped in the back
As she came
He did too
Trying not to speed

## Fleas in Roma

Dusted my ankles
With the poisons
Every evening
Before bedtime

Fleas never bit you
But the lovely sucking—
You kneeled over me
Called me to tongue in you

First showed me your breasts
Then eyes-shut leaned back:
Small touching… now look
No mouth kiss… come tongue in

Oh, I scratched for days
Every welt purpled
Reminded me to
Find you again

a thank you to Making Love
by Mihaly Zichy (Hungary), 1911

## Our best move: we never wed

Please I still want to call in my head yes you your name naked
We had our first time together right by the cool window
The littlest light hairs on your arms and cheeks
We saw down the ivied ravine still dry in early Winter
I'm in love with you still oh am I
In liceo 59 years ago your ear
You were the poetry I whispered
When your soft palm fell onto
The fabric of my pants
Between my legs
Not quite on purpose I thought then
How you were arched in your chair
Your breasts rising
I still want to French kiss
You wouldn't take it in you my
Tongue even while we entered each other
The little sounds we both made
You were one year younger
but now you've died first

## Vittoria

On the street
of the Vomero
my hands were so cold
I pulled on light gloves
to hold your hands.
Somehow yours were warm.
You invited me in
to study matematica.
Once inside, instead,
I pulled you to me,
and your eyes closed.
Instead of kissing, we hugged,
slipping on the couch
covered with plastic.
Your eyes began to roll, and
you asked me to leave right then
before your parents returned.
And as we stood up,
I pulled you to me
once again. I have never felt
another's body soften in that way,
something once called swooning.

## that nap

on vacation in Italia, 1969

"Let's close our eyes," you say. "What do you see?"

I say, "I see our dinner we finish with no wine. I start to
laugh and cannot stop. Why? You look at me, surprised—
the whole restaurant falls silent. I take your hand, and
we come up to our hotel room. When you take off your
blouse, I reach to touch your breasts and you lean toward
me. I put my lips on your left nipple. "Close your eyes,"
you tell me. I do.You straddle me and pull me into you.
You move slowly, as much side-to-side as up-and-down.
And you tell me about the door edge… how you moved
against it when you were young. I put my hands around
your waist, barely touching. Kiss me, I ask."
I cannot hold back.

You say, "I see myself rubbing up and down against the flat
edge of my childhood bedroom door opened. Now when
you touch me a little bit harder, yes, there, I see myself
rubbing again. And when you take my breast with your
lips and pull just a bit, I open my eyes and see that you've
opened yours, too. "Close your eyes," I ask. You do, I do,
and I pull you into me. I want to move quickly, but I don't
and rock side-to-side. I tell you how I rubbed against the
door edge, how wonderful it was. I kept rubbing then, and
I keep moving, now more quickly, and I move up-and-
down. You circle my waist and I feel just the tips of your
fingers there. I want to lean closer to you and I do. I move.
You move, too. I feel you tighten and know that you've
come to me. You plead, "Kiss me."
I kiss you and stay kissing.
Why did you laugh and laugh at dinner?

## like softening eggplants

We touch. We are two softening eggplants, those large berries, what shining complexions. "Sometimes," you whisper, "I see our other colorings, if our aubergine, our melanzana, is cooked just so, to keep that gorgeous tonal sheen." "Is it dark, black?" I ask. You kiss me, and say "No it is a night sky deep azure, an undeniable purple, as when your friends cook it into the parmigiana. That savor sealed the evening for me. My crush on you was heated, sweet with salt, not sugar." "That's how we met," I remember, "a purple favor."

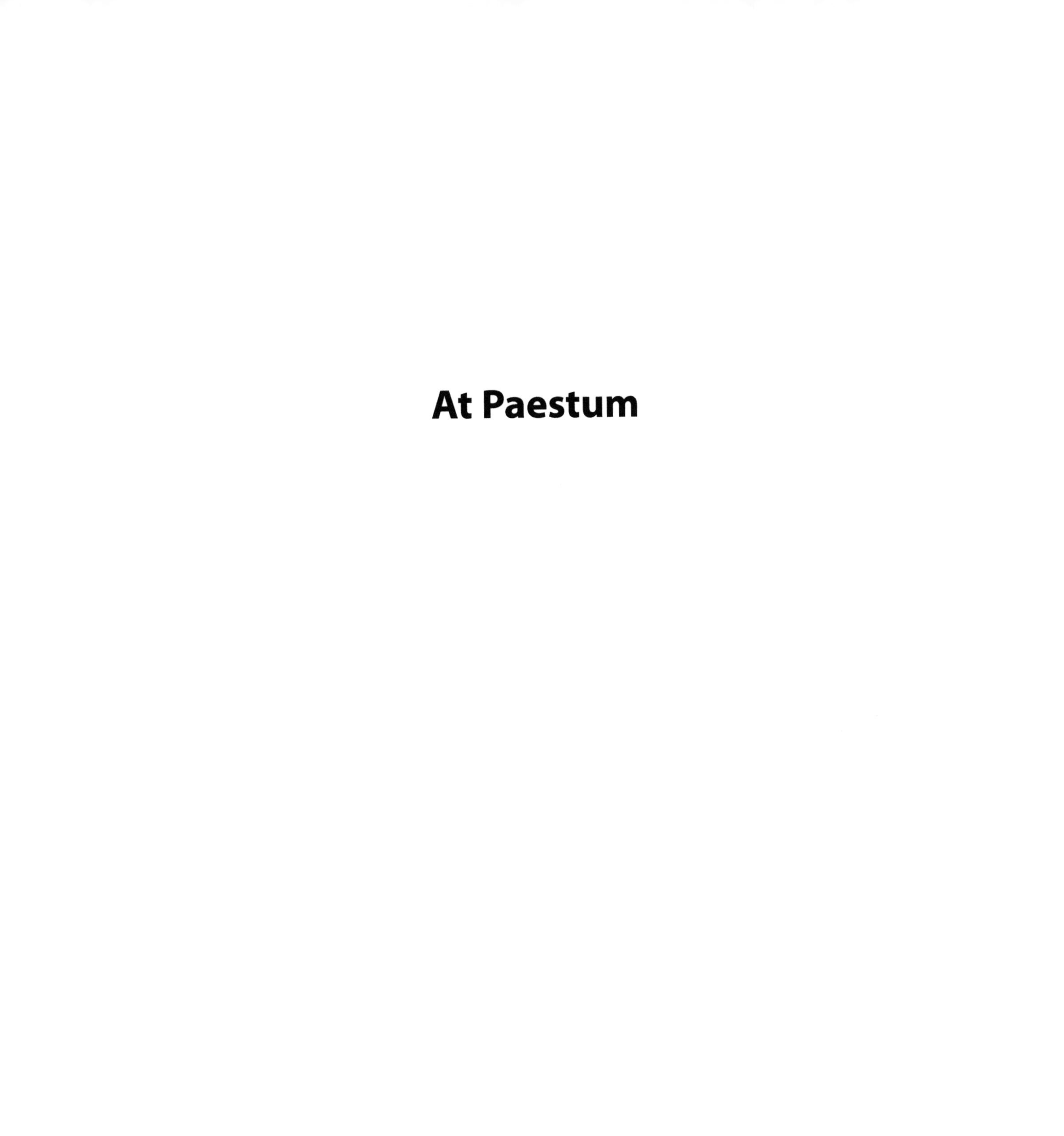

# At Paestum

## At Paestum

a Greek painting

When dying is diving into,
the arms open at the breast,
spread wide to take back in
sea and sky horizon
blend into a line with no point
and the texture of touch runs off.

## A PAESTUM

dipinto greco

Quando morire è tuffarsi nel,
le braccia aperte inanzi al petto,
allargate per riafferrare dentro
mare e orizzonte di cielo
fusi entro una linea senza un punto
e l'ordito del tocco corre e va.

—Translated by Marco-Rossi-Doria

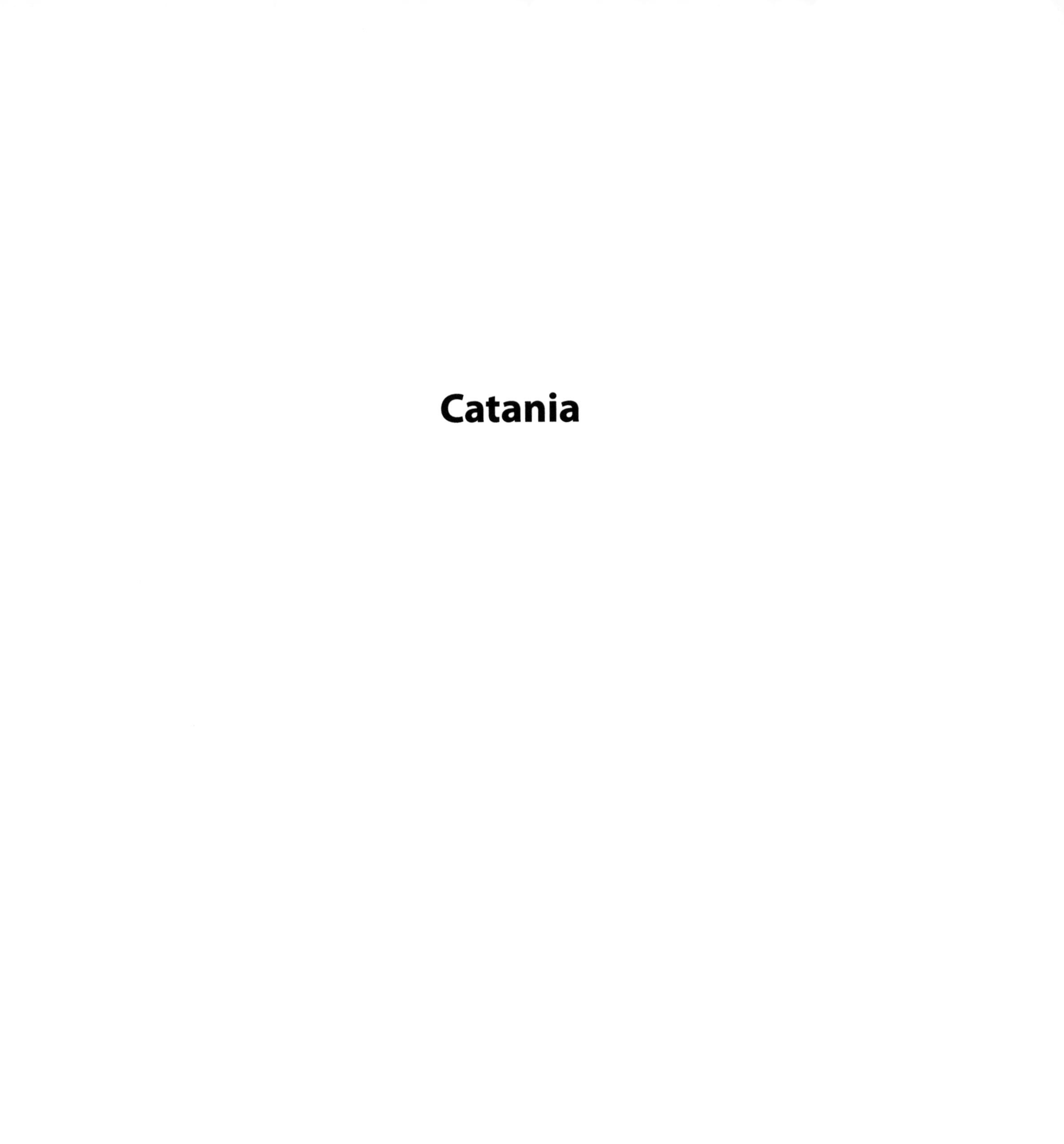

# Catania

## Catania

from Via Etnea

A full two blocks of handles,
stores of shiny handles, elegant knobs,
and the one store of ten thousand blank keys.

•

Taste the nipples first.
the breasts of Sant'Agata—
cinnamon surface

•

Walking in the heat—
watch shirts drying in the breeze
the armpits dry last

•

Pears ripe for picking—
no matter how much we lift
flesh hangs from our bones

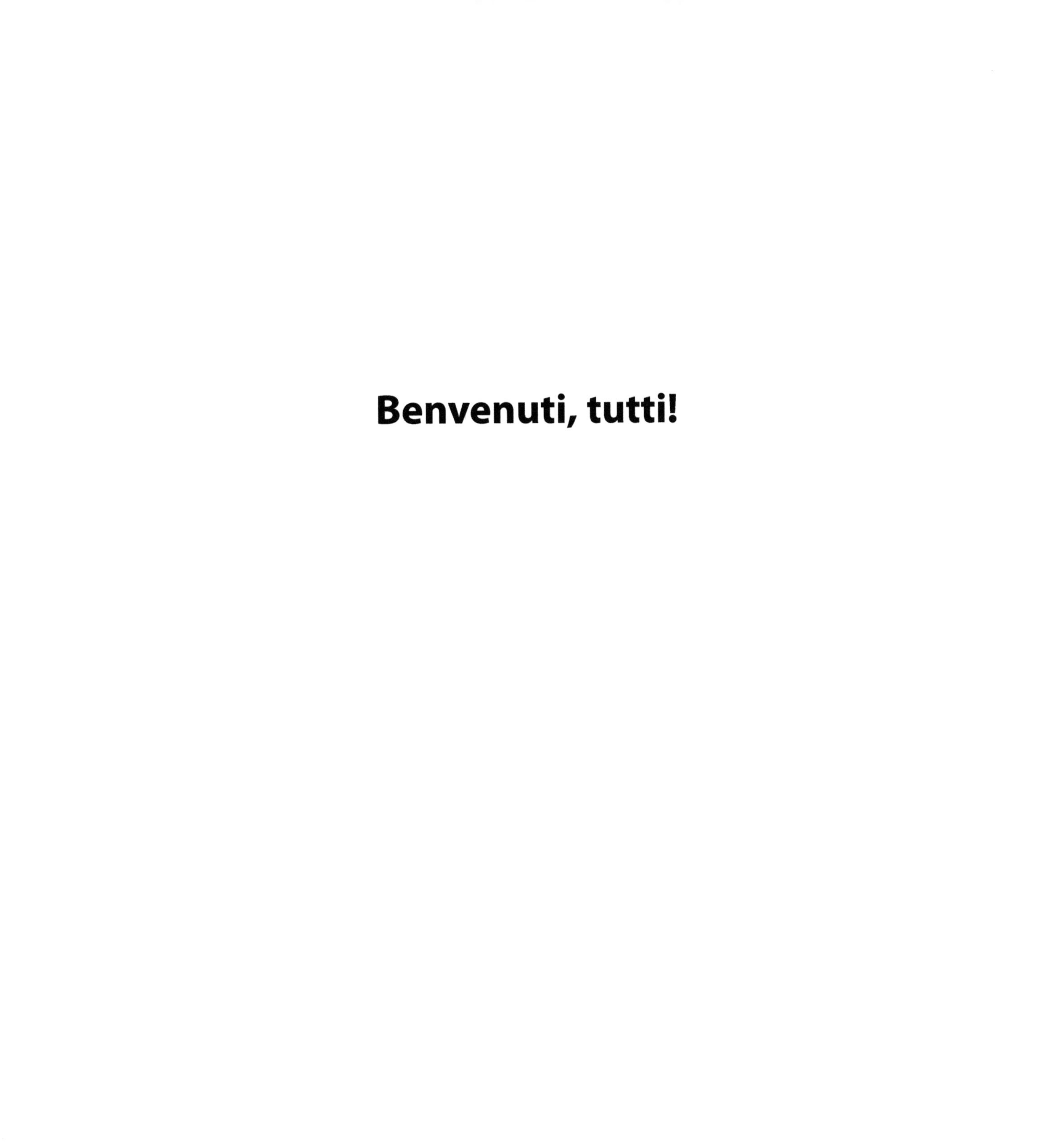
Benvenuti, tutti!

In memory of Anna Tasca Lanza
died July 12, 2010

## Benvenuti, tutti!

Benvenuti, tutti! Welcome everyone! Fifteen years ago my wife and I returned from a sublime winter vacation in Sicilia. Sicilia, homeland to so many different peoples for 10,000 years and to many Americans right now, a homeland not exactly mine, but a homeland in my heart. I must tell you that I am considering changing my name… to… Misterbianco. Please say it with me, Mister Bianco. Funny name, Misterbianco, Mister White: it's actually a town on the lower slopes of the volcano, Etna, the largest live volcano in Europe, covered with winter snow as we saw flying in from the west, but then, no snow visible, with the cloud-cover on the east as we drove from the Catania airport on the Tangenziale to the Circonvallazione CT, the rim road circling around the grand City of Catania, mad traffic all around us.

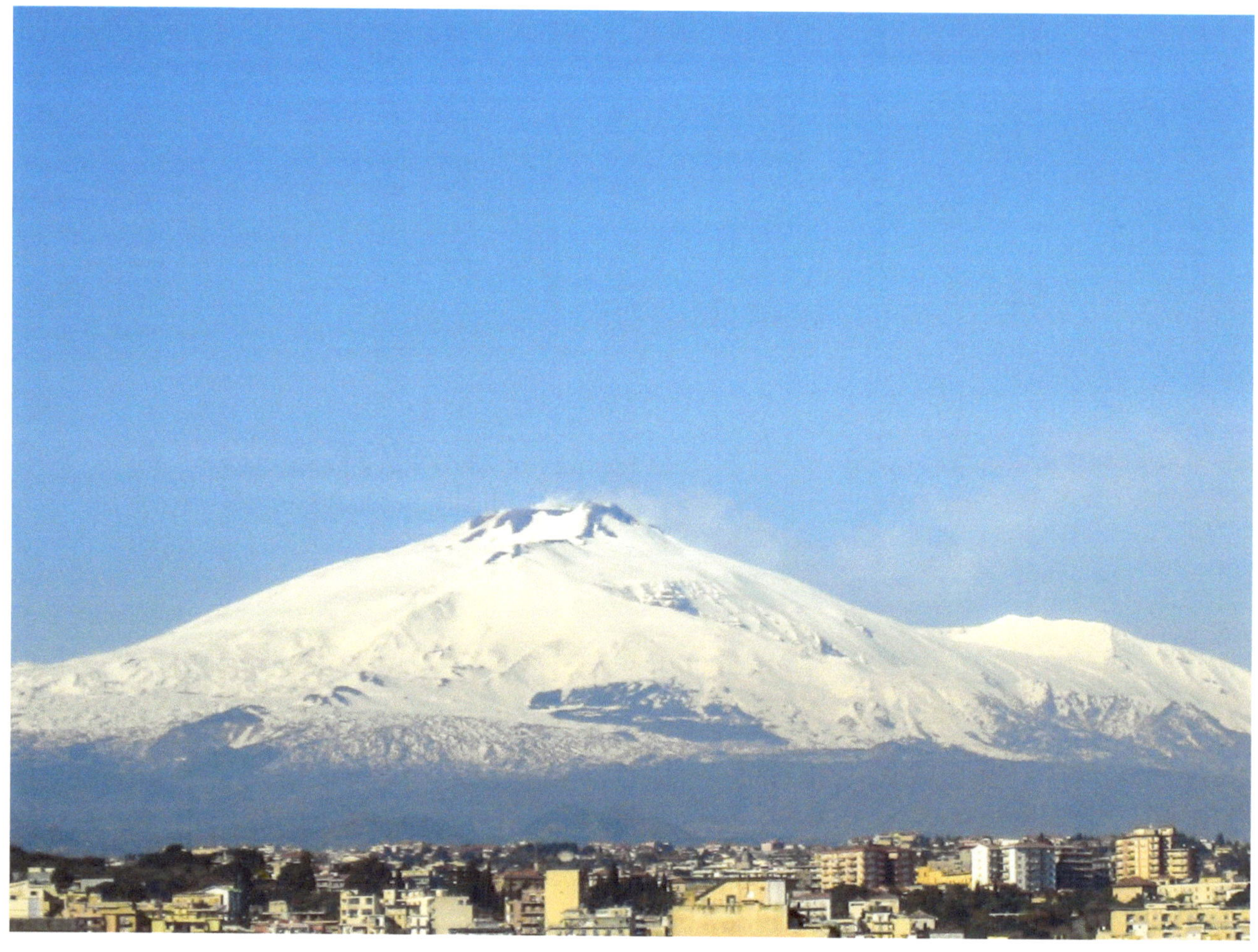

Misterbianco, it could mean white mystery. So I thought. Appropriate, too, when there is snow on the mountain, a headless monster covered with a white vest, il saio bianco. In English, though, I try hard not to think of R. Crumb's Whiteman, Mister Bianco, uptight asshole who finally loosened up by escaping civilization and engaging in some positions not for public consumption, not a bad idea that, but impossible I am sure; that is, impossible to escape civilization.
Heh, heh. Misterbianco, population 44,695, a town on its own with several lovely baroque buildings, but also a sobborgo di Catania, a Catanian suburb. Ah, living under a huge live volcano and driving in impossible traffic

into and out of Catania to work each and every day. Sublime!
In fact, however, the name Misterbianco derives from the Sicilian term Musteri jancu, that means "monastero bianco" (white monastery), and it refers to the white walls of a pre-existent Benedictine monastery, destroyed in the large 1669 eruption, by Mount Etna's lava flow.
Okay then. But before I rush off to the Franz Kafka Meta-Memorial Name-Change Bureau, to don my new name, Misterbianco, I want to tell you one story from the middle of our trip.
After adventures in Catania and on the East Coast of Sicilia, we drove our rented car toward the center of Sicilia, to its heartland. We were to take cooking lessons from the great chef and writer, the Marchesa Anna Tasca Lanza of Regaleali, a Country Estate, yes, but also a fine, fine winery, run by her brother, handed down from his father. Regaleali does not sound exactly Italian so it must be a Sicilian word meaning 'regal.' Right? Way wrong. It is from the Arab rahal Ali meaning village (or home) of Ali. Whoa, there, Sicilia, what of your heritage over these 10,000 years. The Arabs came in the midst of the 1st millennium CE and left so much. One thing they absolutely left was the sweet-and-the-sour in the amazing Sicilian cuisine. So the Marchesa emphasized in her lessons. But wait, I have forgotten to tell you that as we drove over the autostrada and then onto a smaller road and then a narrower lane of potholes and curves, it began to snow. We began to climb, and it began to snow some more. Okay, this is Winter, but this is also Sicilia, and we were not in what Sicilia calls its mountains. But it snowed. And it snowed. And we called the Marchesa on our cellphone: she said the roads were fine, and we'd get through. We drove, and it snowed, and they started to get slippery, and we called again. We talked to her husband, Vincens. We were getting close now, but we were at a fork that he couldn't quite recognize from our description. Finally, somehow, though their directions were not quite there, we arrived at the Estate, at Regaleali. It snowed through our lovely dinner that she prepared and I watched her prepare. And it snowed the next day. She had never seen snow like this at Regaleali in her 72 years, nor heard of it snowing like this, and her family had been there for 175 years. That night we ate a lovely baked chicken covered with herbs collected from the Estate and dried and basted, alternating with orange juice and white wine, the sweet and the sour; and for dessert we had Biancomangiare (white eat), a dish that some think the French brought to Sicilia as Blancmange, a pudding, in Britain, that makes a school boy gag. In fact, Biancomangiare is delicious and simple, sugar, almond milk, and cornstarch with additions of, perhaps, candied squash, coffee, pistachios, vanilla cookies, and certainly cinammon. In fact, these puddings were and are very popular throughout the Middle East, and it is most likely that Biancomangiare came to Sicilia with the Arabs. It is an overwhelming white pudding with little colors of sweet and tangy flavors sitting in and poking out. In the snowy, now icy, night, it was perfection. By now, too, we were snowed in. The Marchesa and her husband were more amazed than we. She had lived there for 70+ years, and it had never snowed like this! I had not slept so well, so deeply, in years. Safe in the warm beds, filled inside with Biancomangiare, snowed in.

Late last night snowed in,
we could go nowhere
but into our dreams
in the darkest rooms.
Sometime near the dawn,
one of us awoke
the other with love,
perhaps our bodies
or even a thought
sent between our two minds
like an icicle
after cracking, still.

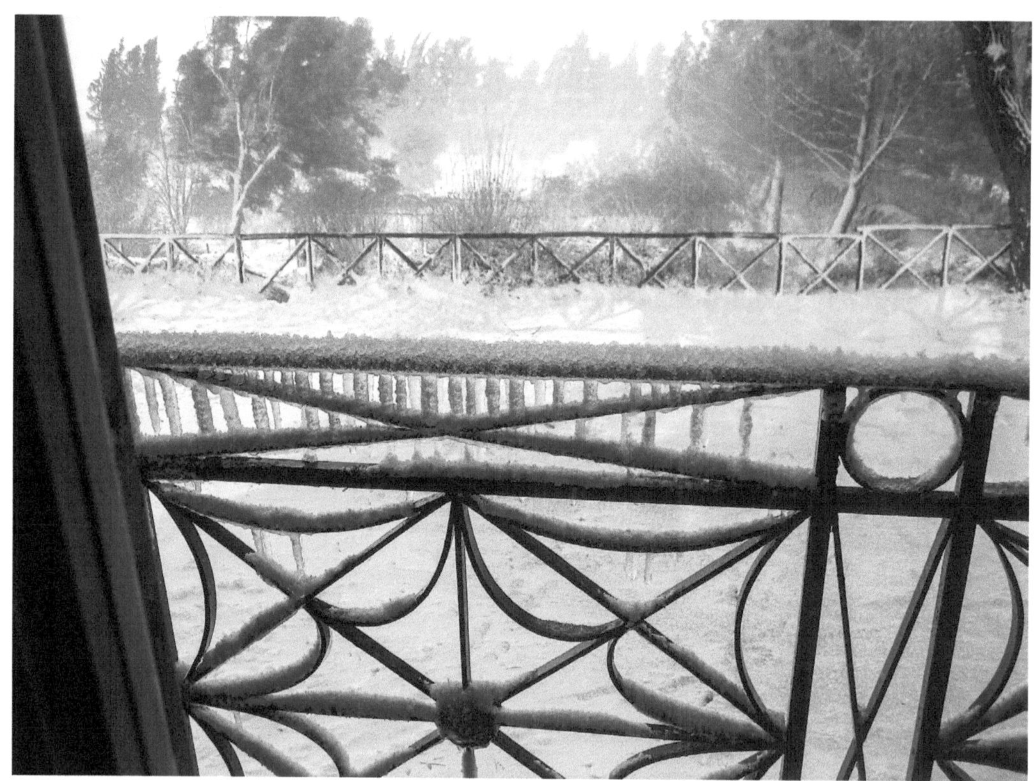

**sway**

# sway

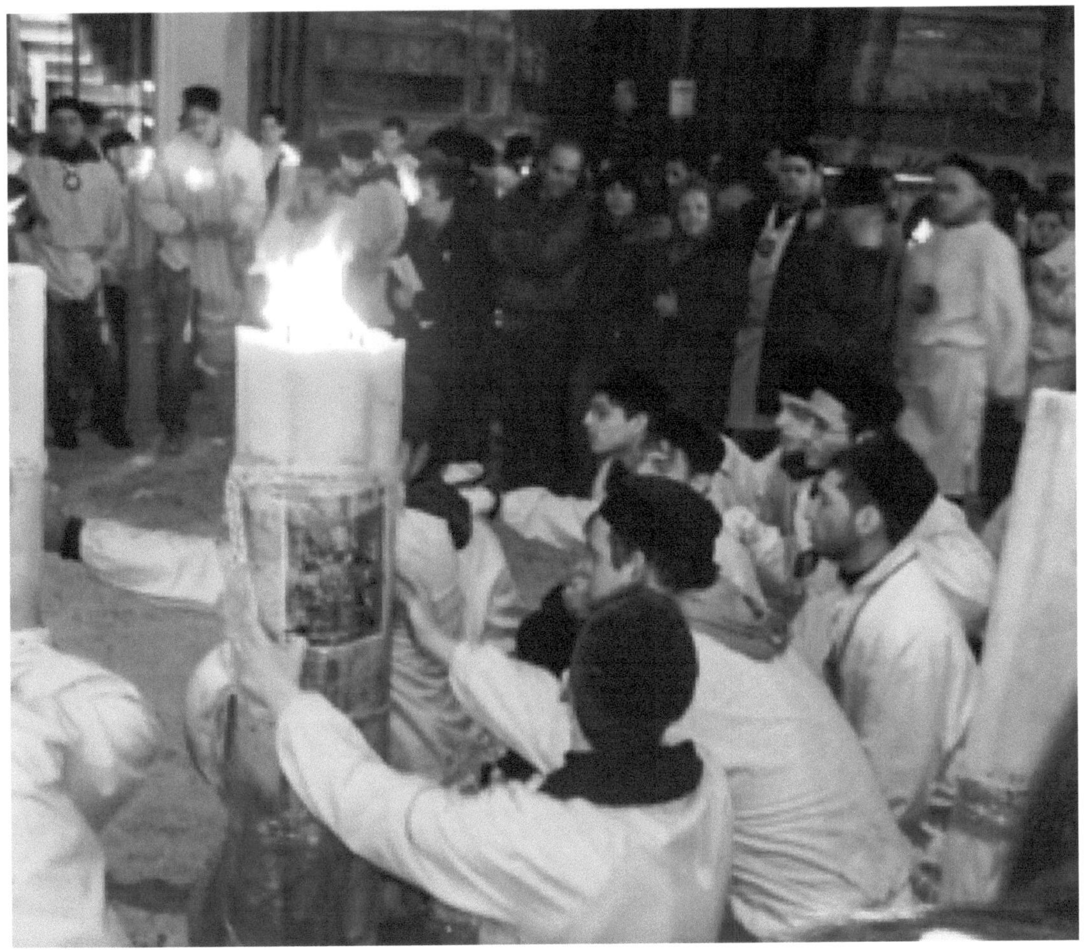

sometimes at night
some nights
waking into silence
that sounds to a thrum
one more invitation out
to walk head held up
but looking down too

onto cobblestones
per forza dewdamp
warm in the latenight
still
before the cold-
before-dawn
coming upon
the many whiteshirts
who lean together
even threes

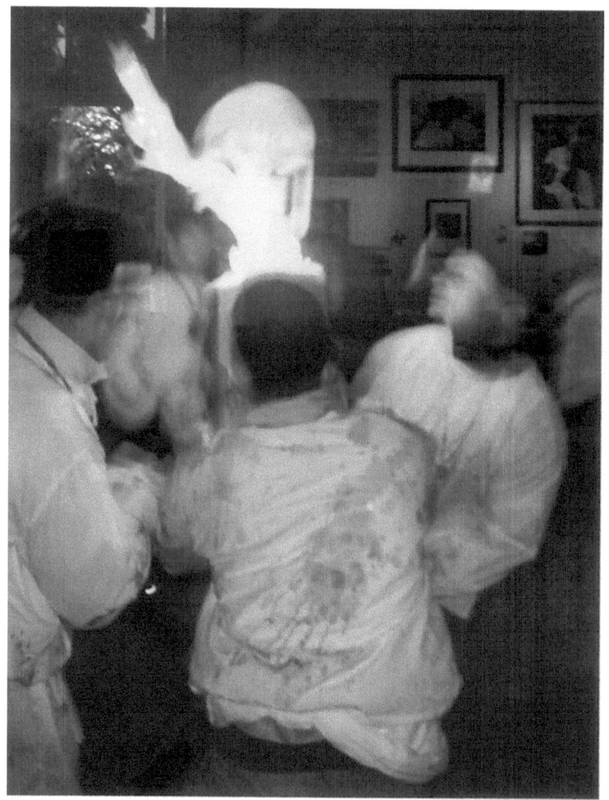

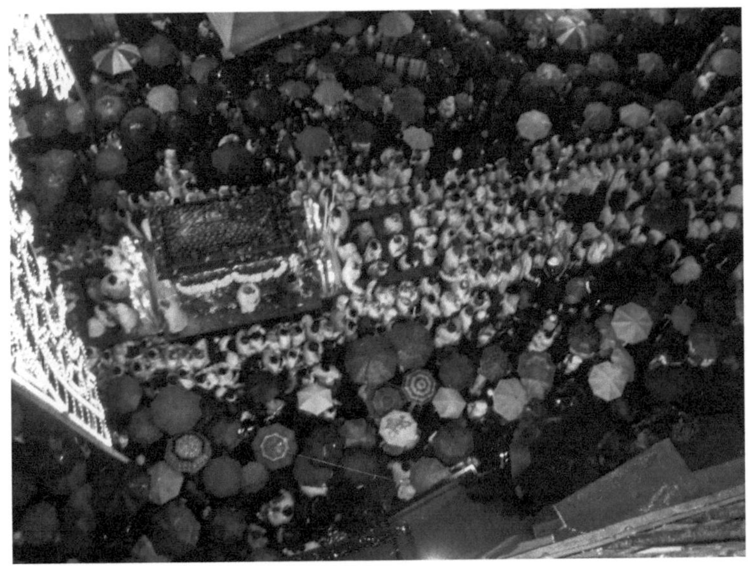

head-to-head-to-head
the fours holding shoulders
in a walking line
never slower
swaying
it cannot be slower
walking without this
swaying
what terrible momentum
unforgiving forward
now stopped
and then
againagainagainagainagainagain
sway
as if
motion
were speaking
low-lowly
ever slower stopping
the ever-swaying
sway

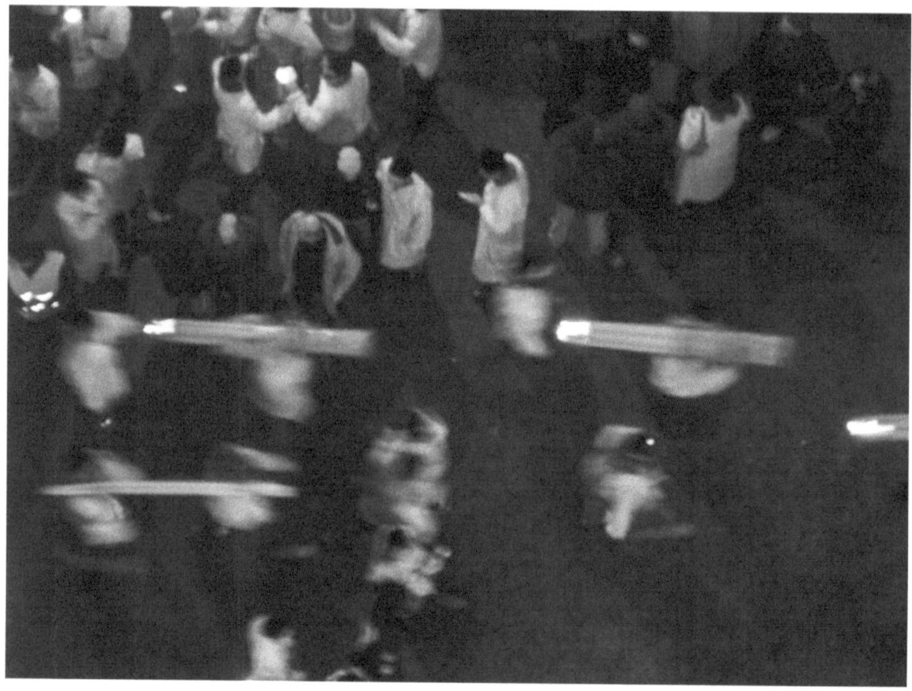

never walked more slowly in such sleepiness    warm this Catanian winter middlenight no rain forecast for the Festa di Sant'Agata    predict the future obstacles nevermind just walk    all the way to the funeral cart down the most dangerous streets    meet it coming on slowly toward pulled by the hundred-and-more whiteshirts ropes through their arms arms also touching linked arms about face to see the cart coming behind then slowing to a near crawl a swaying to stay inching forward the goal already met just ahead also perfect in the side-to-side walk without distance no different than standing an endless ending

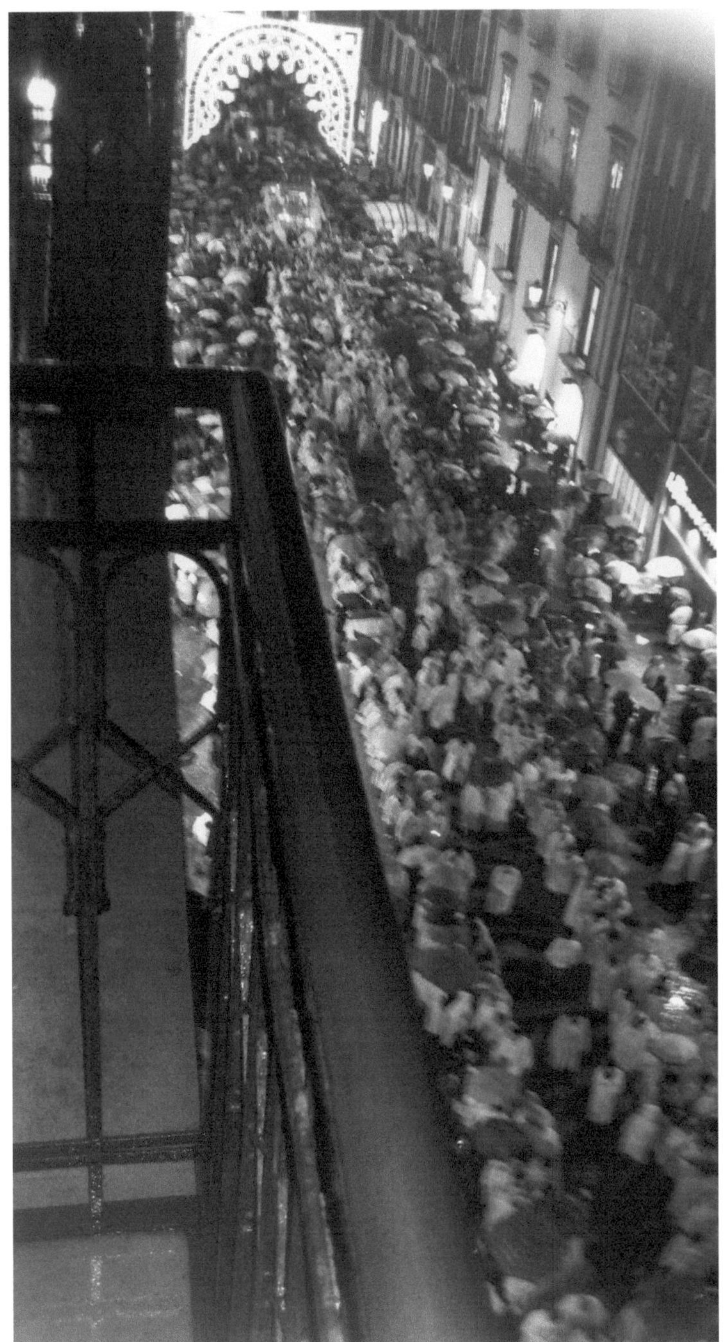

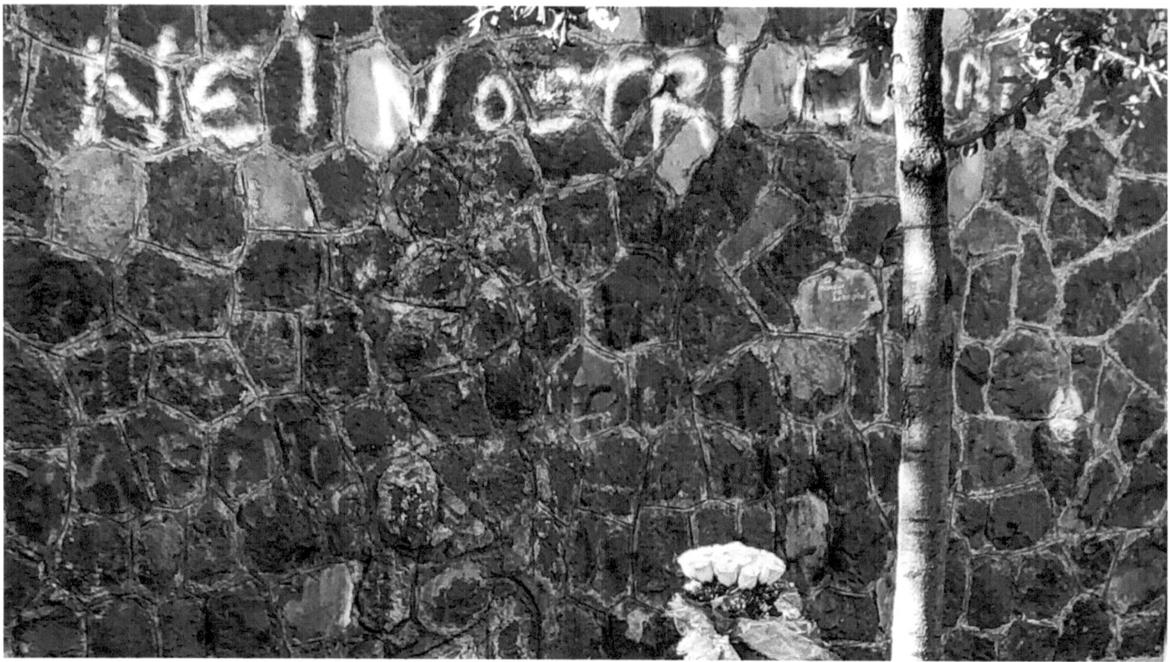

# Thanks & Acknowledgments

Thank you, Rusty Morrison, for your compassionate support of my work and for helping to shape it and sharpen it so beautifully. I am so fortunate to have worked with you on this book!

Thanks, friend Pete Truskier, for shepherding the images through to their final state.

So many thanks to the kind and generous publishers of this book, Dianne Pearce and David Yurkovich of Current Words Publishing.

All photos in *Dreams of the return* were taken by the author.

Cover photo taken in Napoli in November 2018: published as "a Genius volcano," the minison zine, ISSUE 16, AUGUST, MYTHOLOGICAL MINISON, VOLUME 2, p. 18 https://theminisonproject.files.wordpress.com/2022/08/mz-issue-16.pdf

Epigraph for the book is from a Lines & Faces broadside, translated by the author, https://static1.squarespace.com/static/578bbb8bb8a79bbf14deccd7/t/614cf18813a3cf57f79d2071/1632432523777/I%2C2sbit.jpg

Thanks to the Editors of Aletheia Literary Quarterly for their suggestions for the photos of The Loon's Necklace. Photos taken in Matera, United States, and Berlin.

Photos in The Short Day's Dark were taken in Napoli in November 2018.

"Al poco giorno e al gran cerchio d'ombra" (Dante's poem in public domain), translation first published as a Lines & Faces printed broadside, now out of print and an image of broadside shown here:
https://static1.squarespace.com/static/578bbb8bb8a79bbf14deccd7/t/57962e9037c58136e65ecd52/1469460115905/sestina2.jpg
Translation republished by The Hyacinth Review:
https://hyacinthreview.org/alan-bern-al-poco-giorno-e-al-gran-cerchio-dombra-dante-alighieri/

"o Dante" (Dante's poem in public domain), imitation and image published by Last Leaves, Issue 4 (2022), pp. 70-71https://www.lastleavesmag.com/_files/ugd/dccfc8_47d79ed7ed1e4a05ac0ffe963630402e.pdf

"L'infinito" (Leopardi's poem in public domain), translation first published by REUNION: The Dallas Review, Volume 9, 2019. Translation and image reprinted by The Hyacinth Review: https://hyacinthreview.org/alan-bern-linfinito/

"Il Sabato del villaggio" (Leopardi's poem in public domain), translation first published by REUNION: The Dallas Review, Volume 9, 2019

"A se stesso" (Leopardi's poem in public domain), translation first published by REUNION: The Dallas Review, Volume 9, 2019

"Alla Luna" translation published by Southern Arizona Press, *The Stars and Moon in the Evening Sky*, p. 166-7, https://www.southernarizonapress.com/static/1211392ed86d6aa676d712672c55e571/star-and-moon-in-the-evening-sky.pdf?dl=1

Marco Rossi-Doria's poems, AS A DEDICATION and TE L'HO DETTO, are from his book *LA STRADA DELLE ANNURCHE: Poesie* (1973-2020), Studium edizioni (2023), translations by the Alan Bern and Marco Ross-Doria

"after Neapolitan Mass / Caravaggio's The Seven Works of Mercy" appeared in *Poetic Bond IX* (2019), http://www.willowdown-books.com/thepoeticbond.html

"The Good One," photo taken in Napoli in 2009. Published in a different version by *Iris Literary Journal, Volume 2 Issue 1*. https://assurepress.org/irislitjournal

"See Naples and Die" was first published in *Waterwalking in Berkeley* (Fithian Press, 2007). It was republished by *MEDITERRANEAN POETRY, May 21, 2021*, https://www.odyssey.pm/contributors/alan-bern/ Translation by Marco Rossi-Doria

"Pavese encircling," in a different version, published by *Porridge Magazine, Issue 7, 2024*. https://porridgemagazine.com, photos taken at Sacro Monte di Crea in 2009

Some of the poems from "San Francesco d'Assisi" were originally published, some in different versions, in Alan Bern's second book of poetry, *Waterwalking in Berkeley* (Fithian Press, 2007). Photos taken in the Sacro Monte di Orta

The final part of "Cantico di Frate Sole" or "Cantico delle Creature"
https://hyacinthreview.org/alan-bern-cantico-di-frate-sole-or-cantico-delle-creature/
This piece was also part of *PACES: dance & poetry fit to the space* performance DIVINING TRIPTYCHS, which can be viewed at https://www.youtube.com/watch?v=MKzGNF4g4Lg and https://www.youtube.com/watch?v=M_n_0uMKfTo

Translation of "The Wolf of Gubbio" by Marco Rossi-Doria

"from several stations in the Leggenda di San Francesco d'Assisi by Giotto di Bondone" won the Littoral Press Poetry Prize in 2015 and was reprinted by Southern Arizona Press in *Castles and Courtyards: A poetic anthology celebrating the medieval life of kings, queens, peasants, and troubadours by poetic bards from across the globe*, p. 102
https://www.southernarizonapress.com/static/dee8b3dcb82eca7fee369d737cf1a186/castles-and-courtyards-final-2.pdf?dl=1

The prose poem "like softening eggplants" was first published in a different version by *FAIRY PIECE MAG! in Issue 5 – Summer 2022*, https://fairypiecemag.wordpress.com/alan-bern/

"Vittoria" was first published in *Waterwalking in Berkeley* (Fithian Press, 2007).

"At Paestum" and "Catania" were first published in *Waterwalking in Berkeley* (Fithian Press, 2007). Both were republished by *MEDITERRANEAN POETRY, May 21, 2021*, https://www.odyssey.pm/contributors/alan-bern/ Translation of "At Paestum" by Marco Rossi-Doria

"Benvenuti tutti!" was first published in *Solstice: A Winter Anthology (The Solstice Winter Anthology Series), Volume 2 – November 30, 2022.*

Photos taken in Catania and at Case Vecchie in Sicilia in 2006

Without the photos, "sway" was a semi-finalist in *Naugatuck River Review's 10th Narrative Poetry Contest*. It was republished by *MEDITERRANEAN POETRY, May 21, 2021*, https://www.odyssey.pm/contributors/alan-bern/

Photos in "sway" taken by the author at Festa di Sant'Agata in Catania in 2006

Other photo images:

"Rivering" (p. 94) taken in Catania at the Festa di Sant'Agata in 2006 and "Taking off from Pebbles" (p. 10) taken in San Anselmo, California in 2019:

"The candles of Sant'Agata" (p. 91) https://wanderlust-journal.com/2021/07/27/the-candles-of-santagata/

"Festa di Sant Agata Catania" (p.93), *The Courtship of Winds, Summer 2023* https://www.thecourtshipofwinds.org

The photo "NEI NOSTRI CUORI" (p. 98) taken in Catania in 2006

Bern slides between two worlds trying to triangulate where he is and what is happening, translating Italian into English, while his own poems are translated into Italian. His journey of remembrance and reckoning takes him back again and again to those age-old questions raised so long ago in Naples. Yes, there are side trips, north to Assisi and Orta, love poems along the way, but this book chronicles the return of Alan's psyche to Italy's south, magical, mysterious, magnificent.

Stephen Tobriner
Professor Emeritus of Architectural History and Italian
University of California Berkeley

///

For decades I've asked myself: why in the world, after just one year in an Italian high school, has Alan Bern wanted, again and again, through his whole life, to nourish his attachment to Napoli and to keep himself fully and kindly loyal to Italian? Now we are two old men. And I sometimes think that it is not Alan who has kept my Neapolitan places within him so richly, completely. Rather, it may be the other way around. It may be that this language full of music and Napoli old and powerful have decided to keep reaching out for Alan, month after month, year after year, all the way across the Mediterranean and through Gibraltar, the Atlantic Ocean, the Great Plains, the Rocky Mountains, the Sierras, to him in Berkeley.

Marco Rossi-Doria, author of *LA STRADA DELLE ANNURCHE, Poesie* (1973-2020), and President of the *Si Cambia Association*

## About the author

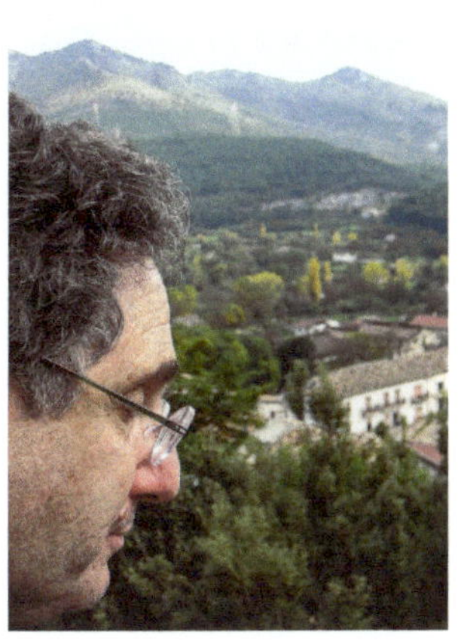

Retired children's librarian Alan Bern received an MA in Creative Writing from Boston University studying with poet Anne Sexton and classicist Donald Carne-Ross. Alan is a Pushcart nominee and has published three books of poetry and a hybrid fictionalized memoir, *IN THE PACE OF THE PATH, UnCollected Press*, 2023. Alan has a chapbook, because lack, forthcoming from back room poetry in June 2024, https://backroompoetry.co.uk. Recent awards include: Longlist, The Bedford Competition (2023); Winner, Saw Palm Poetry Contest (2022). Recent/upcoming writing and photo work include: *Third Street Review, EcoTheo Review, Thanatos, The Hyacinth Review, DarkWinter, Feral, Porridge Magazine,* and *Mercurius*. Alan performs with dancer/choreographer Lucinda Weaver as *PACES: dance & poetry fit to the space*, is a published/exhibited photographer, and runs a fine press/publisher with artist/printer Robert Woods, *Lines & Faces:* linesandfaces.com.

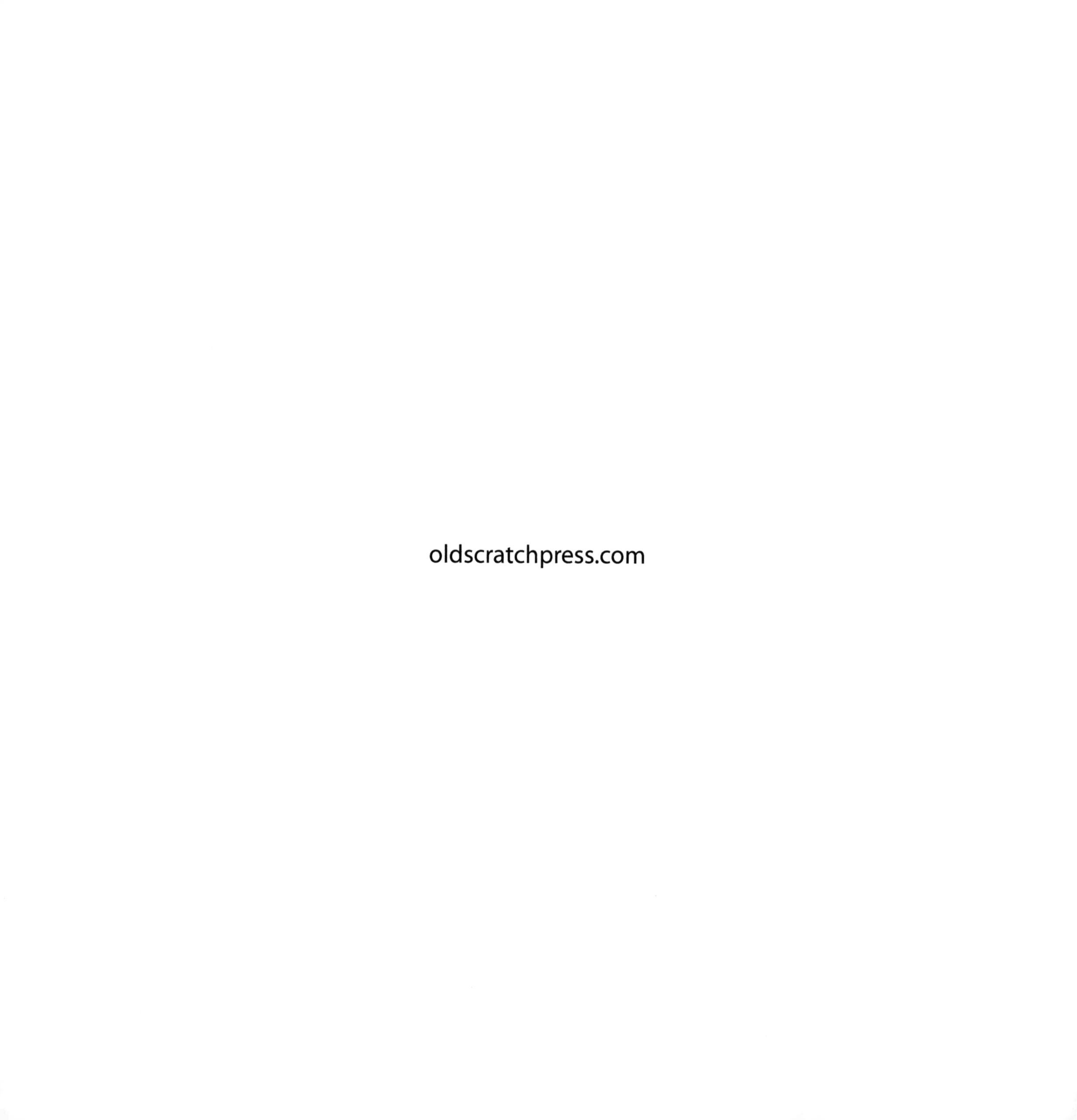

oldscratchpress.com

www.ingramcontent.com/pod-product-compliance
Ingram Content Group UK Ltd.
Pitfield, Milton Keynes, MK11 3LW, UK
UKHW060101300726
14090UKWH00003B/337

* 9 7 8 1 9 5 7 2 2 4 9 0 9 *